Anonymous

Improved Question-book

And Studies on the Parables and other Instructions of the Saviour

Anonymous

Improved Question-book
And Studies on the Parables and other Instructions of the Saviour

ISBN/EAN: 9783744758826

Printed in Europe, USA, Canada, Australia, Japan

Cover: Foto ©Paul-Georg Meister /pixelio.de

More available books at **www.hansebooks.com**

QUESTION-BOOK,

AND

STUDIES

ON THE

PARABLES AND OTHER INSTRUCTIONS
OF THE SAVIOUR.

WITH THE TEXT.

ARRANGED FOR CLASSES OF ALL AGES.

PHILADELPHIA:
AMERICAN SUNDAY-SCHOOL UNION,
No. 1122 Chestnut Street.

New York: Nos, 8 & 10 Bible House, Astor Place.

Entered according to Act of Congress, in the year 1871, by the
AMERICAN SUNDAY-SCHOOL UNION,
In the Office of the Librarian of Congress, at Washington.

PREFACE.

The excellence of the system of instruction on which these books are founded is now so universally admitted, that there is no reason for detailing its advantages.

The questions might have been easily increased to a much larger number on each lesson; but such an increase would be unprofitable to the schools. When a person asks *all* the questions which may occur to his own mind, there must necessarily be many of an indirect character, the appropriateness of which would not be seen by others. *The great object of a book of questions is, to excite the mind to a careful and thorough examination of the Scriptures.* When the mind is once aroused and led forward in the right course, it receives no benefit from being burdened with too many questions. Too many questions also render the instruction mechanical, and prevent the teacher from the exercise of his own powers. It should also be remembered that these Question-Books are intended for teachers as well as scholars: therefore it may be expected that questions and references will occasionally be found which are rather designed to help the teacher in *explaining*, than the class in learning. And whenever a question is not easily understood by the scholar, it should be simplified by the teacher.

EXPLANATIONS.

The figures placed at the beginning of the lines denote the several verses of Scripture constituting the lesson.

The questions are printed in large and in small type. The answers to those which are printed in large type are very plain and consist of the *whole*, or a *portion*, of the verse. The answers to the questions in smaller type serve more fully to explain and apply the lesson.

Mode of Teaching.—The teacher should ascertain that his scholars are well acquainted with the lesson, and should require each pupil to repeat the verses distinctly and accurately from memory. Then he may ask them the questions, or as many of them as he pleases,—always taking care that when a question is asked of one scholar, the rest of the class are listening. Teachers should take pains to explain the meaning of each verse, and ask many questions which are not in the book.

Teachers' Meetings.—Wherever it is practicable, the teachers will derive great benefit from meeting together once a week, for the purpose of examining the lesson for the ensuing Sabbath.

Dividing Lessons.—In some cases it may be expedient to divide a lesson and spend two weeks on it. The superintendent should make the division, in such case, and give notice of it to the school. Care should be taken that all the classes have the same lesson.

References.—Scholars and teachers should be encouraged to look out the Scripture references, and show that they understand their application to the subject.

It is not necessary in every case that they should repeat them; many passages being referred to for information which can be gained from them without reading the whole passage.

Monthly Review.—Those who think proper, can spend every *fourth* Sabbath in reviewing the lessons of the three preceeding weeks. No one class in a school should do this unless the others adopt the same plan; for it is of great importance that all the classes should have the same lesson.

Ministers.—It is of vital importance to the success of Sunday-schools that ministers of the gospel should watch over them and see that all things are conducted with propriety. Many clergymen give weekly lectures on the portion of Scripture which is to be the lesson for the ensuing Sabbath. This is found very useful.

Question-Books.—Every family should own a question-book. It is expected that the scholars will study their lessons during the week. If they have a book at home, they can receive aid from their parents. Children are often greatly assisted by their parents and elder brothers and sisters.

Family Instruction.—Most families who are sufficiently near to a Sunday-school will find it good to send their children. But there are some families who are so situated that their children cannot be connected with any school. Some parents, who are thus situated, have introduced a system of teaching their children on the Sabbath, either *before* or *after* the time of public worship.

In studying the lessons, both teachers and scholars will derive great help from several works published by the American Sunday-School Union, prepared for the purpose.

PARABLES

AND OTHER

INSTRUCTIONS OF THE SAVIOUR.

LESSON I.

Christ's Conversation with Nicodemus.

JOHN iii. 1-12.

1 There was a man of the Pharisees, named Nicodemus, a ruler of the Jews:
2 The same came to Jesus by night, and said unto him, Rabbi, we know that thou art a teacher come from God: for no man can do these miracles that thou doest, except God be with him.
3 Jesus answered and said unto him, Verily, verily, I say unto thee, Except a man be born again, he cannot see the kingdom of God.
4 Nicodemus saith unto him, How can a man be born when he is old? can he enter the second time into his mother's womb, and be born?
5 Jesus answered, Verily, verily, I say unto thee, Except a man be born of water and of the Spirit, he cannot enter into the kingdom of God.
6 That which is born of the flesh is flesh; and that which is born of the Spirit is spirit.
7 Marvel not that I said unto thee, Ye must be born again.
8 The wind bloweth where it listeth, and thou hearest the sound thereof, but canst not tell whence it cometh, and whither it goeth: so is every one that is born of the Spirit.
9 Nicodemus answered and said unto him, How can these things be?
10 Jesus answered and said unto him, Art thou a master of Israel, and knowest not these things?
11 Verily, verily, I say unto thee, We speak that we do know, and testify that we have seen; and ye receive not our witness.
12 If I have told you earthly things, and ye believe not, how shall ye believe, if I tell you of heavenly things?

1. WHO is here spoken of?
What office did he hold?
What was the character of the Pharisees? (They were, as a body, self-righteous, and proud of their strict observance of the outward duties of religion.)
What is a ruler? (One who superintended and directed the worship of the synagogue.)

2. To whom did Nicodemus come?
At what time?
What did he say to him?
What is the meaning of *Rabbi?*—John i. 38.

Why did Nicodemus think that Jesus was a teacher who had come from God?
What are miracles? (Effects performed by supernatural power.)
Who alone can give power to work miracles? (God.)
On what occasions had Jesus been working miracles?—John ii. 11, 23.

3. How did Jesus answer Nicodemus?
What is the meaning of *verily?* (Truly.)
What is it to see the kingdom of God? (To enter into it, to enjoy its blessings.)
What is the kingdom of God? (Christ's spiritual church on earth; or the holy and happy place prepared in heaven for those that love him.)

4. What did Nicodemus ask Jesus?
Did he understand Jesus aright? (No.)

5. How did Jesus again answer him?
Who is the Spirit? (The third Person of the Trinity.)
What is it to be born of water and of the Spirit?
Why is this called being "born again"? (It is the beginning of a new and of a spiritual life.)
By what other names is it called?—See Titus iii. 5.
What is man's duty to God?—Deut. vi. 5.
Are men naturally disposed to do this? (No.)—Job xxi. 14, 15.
Must not then their hearts be *changed* before they will love God? (Yes.)—Rom. viii. 7.
Who makes this change? (God.)
What makes this a great encouragement to seek for a change of heart?—Ezek. xviii. 31, 32.
How does the apostle encourage this?—Phil. ii. 12, 13.
How can you know if you are born of the Spirit, and thus fitted to enter the kingdom of God?—1 John iii. 9, 10.

6. What are the words of the Lord Jesus in this verse?
What does this mean? (We are all, by nature, sinful, and can be changed only through the influence of the Holy Spirit.)

7. What else did Jesus tell Nicodemus?
What is it to *marvel?* (To wonder.)
If men are not born again, what must become of them?—Psalm ix. 17.

8. To what did Jesus compare this?
What is the meaning of listeth? (Pleases.)
How can you tell that the wind is blowing?
Can you see the wind?
How can you know that a person has been born of the Spirit? (By his conduct.)—Eph. v. 9.

9. Was Nicodemus satisfied yet?
Why could he not understand?—1 Cor. ii. 14.

10. How did Jesus answer him?
What was *a master of Israel?* (A religious teacher.)
Why should a master of Israel know more about these things than others? (He should have learned them from the Old Testament Scriptures, which he professed to teach.)
Where might he have learned this doctrine?—See Ps. li. 10, 11; Ezek. xi. 19.

11. What did Jesus say he spoke and testified?
What is it to *testify?* (To bear witness to.)
What things were these that Jesus had seen?
What things did Jesus know? (The doctrines taught by him in the Gospels.)
Was the witness of Jesus received?
How was it treated?—John viii. 52, 53.

12. Does want of belief prevent our knowledge of important truths?

LESSON II.

Christ's Conversation with Nicodemus, continued.

JOHN iii. 13-21.

13 And no man hath ascended up to heaven, but he that came down from heaven, *even* the Son of man which is in heaven.
14 ¶ And as Moses lifted up the serpent in the wilderness, even so must the Son of man be lifted up:
15 That whosoever believeth in him should not perish, but have eternal life.
16 ¶ For God so loved the world, that he gave his only begotten Son, that whosoever believeth in him should not perish, but have everlasting life.
17 For God sent not his Son into the world to condemn the world; but that the world through him might be saved.
18 ¶ He that believeth on him is not condemned: but he that believeth not is condemned already, because he hath not believed in the name of the only begotten Son of God.
19 And this is the condemnation, that light is come into the world, and men loved darkness rather than light, because their deeds were evil.
20 For every one that doeth evil hateth the light, neither cometh to the light, lest his deeds should be reproved.
21 But he that doeth truth cometh to the light, that his deeds may be made manifest, that they are wrought in God.

13. WHY is no *man* able to "tell of heavenly things" from his own knowledge?
Does this mean that no man had gone to heaven? (No.)—Gen. v. 24; 2 Kings ii. 11.
How does the rest of the verse explain this? (No one has returned from heaven to speak of these things.)
Who *is* able?

What is said here of the Son of man?
Who is meant by the Son of man? (Jesus Christ—in his human nature.)
How was he then in heaven? (In his divine nature.)

14. What did Christ then speak of?
Read the account of this.—Num. xxi. 5-9.
What did God send upon the people of Israel for their sins?
What did he direct Moses to do for their cure?
How was Jesus lifted up? (On the cross.)
What does Jesus say of himself in John xii. 32, 33?
In what respect was that serpent a type of Christ? (All who looked upon it were healed, and lived; as all who look upon Christ with the eye of faith will be purified and obtain eternal life.)

15. Why was he to be lifted up?
What is it to *perish?*—2 Thess. i. 9.
Who shall be saved from perishing?
What shall such receive?
What is eternal life? (Happiness in heaven forever.)
What is it to believe in Christ? (To believe in his divine nature, and in his sacrifice for our sins, and depend on him alone for our salvation.)

16. Why may sinners be saved in this way?
Have men done any thing to deserve this love?—Rom. iii. 11, 12.
What do they deserve?—Ezek. xviii. 4.
Who is the only-begotten Son of God? (Our Lord Jesus Christ.)
How does this show God's love?

17. What was God's design in sending his son?
Will all the world be saved?—Mark xvi. 16.

18. Who shall not be condemned?
Who shall be condemned?
Why?
How does Jesus save those who believe in him?—Gal. iii. 13.
How can one know if he really believes in Jesus?—1 John ii. 3-5.
What is it to believe "in the name of the only-begotten Son of God"? (To believe in him as the only Son of God.)

19. What is the reason of the condemnation of unbelievers?
Who is meant by that Light which is come into the world?—John viii. 12.
What is meant by darkness? (Ignorance and sin.)
Why do men love this darkness?

20. How do they show this?

INSTRUCTIONS OF THE SAVIOUR. 11

Can you mention any of the ways in which persons keep out of the light?
Will it make men safe to keep themselves in ignorance? (No.) —Matt. xxv. 30.
What is the meaning of *reproved?* (Censured, condemned, blamed.)
What is written in Eccl. xii. 14?

21. What is said of him that doeth truth?
What is it to do truth? (To act in obedience to the truth.)
What is it to be *made manifest?* (To be shown plainly.)
How are the works of believers said to be *wrought in God?*—1 Cor. xv. 10.
How does a true believer pray?—Ps. cxxxix. 23, 24.
What are the great doctrines taught in this lesson? (The necessity of regeneration, and the love of God in giving his Son to redeem the world.)
On whom do those believe who are born again?—1 John v. 1.
When do we hear of Nicodemus after this conversation?—See John vii. 45-53; xix. 39.

LESSON III.

Jesus teaches the Nazarenes, and is rejected by them.

LUKE iv. 16-30.

16 ¶ And he came to Nazareth, where he had been brought up; and, as his custom was, he went into the synagogue on the sabbath day, and stood up for to read.
17 And there was delivered unto him the book of the prophet Esaias. And when he had opened the book, he found the place where it was written,
18 The Spirit of the Lord is upon me, because he hath anointed me to preach the gospel to the poor; he hath sent me to heal the broken-hearted, to preach deliverance to the captives, and recovering of sight to the blind, to set at liberty them that are bruised,
19 To preach the acceptable year of the Lord.
20 And he closed the book, and he gave it again to the minister, and sat down. And the eyes of all them that were in the synagogue were fastened on him.
21 And he began to say unto them, This day is this Scripture fulfilled in your ears.
22 And all bare him witness and wondered. at the gracious words which proceeded out of his mouth. And they said, Is not this Joseph's son?
23 And he said unto them, Ye will surely say unto me this proverb, Physician, heal thyself; whatsoever we have heard done in Capernaum, do also here in thy country.
24 And he said, Verily I say unto you, No prophet is accepted in his own country.
25 But I tell you of a truth, many widows were in Israel in the days of Elias, when the heaven was shut up three years and six months, when great famine was throughout all the land;
26 But unto none of them was Elias sent, save unto Sarepta, *a city of* Sidon, unto a woman *that was* a widow.
27 And many lepers were *in* Israel in the time of Eliseus the prophet; and none ot them was cleansed, saving Naaman the Syrian.
28 And all they in the synagogue,

when they heard these things, were filled with wrath.

29 And rose up, and thrust him out of the city, and led him unto the brow of the hill whereon their city was built,

that they might cast him down headlong.

30 But he, passing through the midst of them, went his way.

16. IN the course of his preaching, to what place did Jesus come?
Had he spent any portion of his life there?
As Joseph and Mary lived at Nazareth, how was it that Jesus was born at Bethlehem?—Luke ii. 1-7.
What was he accustomed to do on the Sabbath day?
What was the synagogue? (A place of worship and religious instruction.)
Can you give any account of the Jewish worship in synagogues? (It began with prayer, then portions from the law and the prophets were read, with an address to the people, and it was closed with prayer.)
What books were read in the synagogues on the Sabbath?—Acts xiii. 15, and xv. 21.
Why is it important that we maintain religious worship on the Sabbath? (That we may honour God by observing his ordinances, and that the gospel may be preached.)
What benefits do Christians derive from assembling together? —Matt. xviii. 19, 20.

17. What was given him to read?
By what name is Esaias called in the Old Testament? (Isaiah.)

18. What part of the prophecy did he read?
Where is that to be found?—Isa. lxi. 1, 2.
Upon whom was the Spirit of the Lord? (Upon Jesus.)
What is meant by that? (The Holy Spirit was with him.)
How did Christ show that the Holy Spirit was with him? (By his holy life, his miracles, his fulfilment of the prophecies respecting himself.)
What is written in Luke iii. 22, and iv. 14?
What is meant by his being *anointed* to preach the gospel? (Consecrated by his heavenly Father to that purpose.)
On what occasions was anointing anciently used? (Anointing, or pouring sacred oil on the head, was a ceremony used on the induction into office of a prophet, priest, or king.)
What is the meaning of the words *Christ* and *Messiah?* (The Anointed.)
To whom was Jesus to preach the Gospel?
What is the gospel? (The good tidings of salvation.)
Is the gospel sent to none but the poor?—Mark xvi. 15.
Why do you think they are mentioned particularly? (To show us that there is no respect of persons with God.)
What kind of poor may be meant?—Matt. v. 3.
Whom was Christ sent to heal?

INSTRUCTIONS OF THE SAVIOUR.

What kind of persons are the broken-hearted?—Isa. lxvi. 2.
What is said of the broken-hearted in Ps. xxxiv. 18?
How did he heal such?—Matt. xi. 28-30.

To whom was Christ to preach deliverance?
What *captives* are meant?—2 Tim. ii. 26.
What deliverance had Jesus been sent to preach to them?—Col. i. 13, 14.

What did Christ do for the blind?
What sort of blindness is meant?—Eph. iv. 18.
How does Christ enlighten such?—Acts xxvi. 18.

Whom was he to set at liberty?
Who are meant by the *bruised?* (Broken-hearted by affliction, or by a sense of unfitness.)
How does he set them at liberty? (He gives them peace through faith in his atonement for sin.)

19. What else was Christ to preach?
What is the *acceptable year* of the Lord?—2 Cor. vi. 2.
Where else is this spoken of?—Isa. xlix. 8.
How is that quoted in the New Testament?—2 Cor. vi. 2.
What else is said of Christ in that prophecy?—Isa. xlix. 9, 10.

20. When Jesus had closed the book, what did he do?
Who was called the *minister* of the synagogue?*
What is said of those who were in the synagogue?

21. What did he say to them?
How was that scripture fulfilled in their ears? (By Christ's preaching salvation.)

22. What did they all do?
What is meant by *all bare him witness?* They confessed the wisdom and truth of what he said.)
Why are his words called *gracious?* (They were so wise and kind.)
What did they say?
Why did they ask this question? (They thought that if Jesus were the Messiah, he would not have condescended to so mean a station.)

23. What did he say they would be likely to say to him?
How did this proverb apply to him? (Jesus had worked miracles in other places, and they urged him now to do it in his own city.)
How had he spoken of himself as a physician?—Verse 18.
What was done in Capernaum of which they had heard? (Many miraculous cures.)
Why was Nazareth called his country?—Matt. ii. 23.

---

* See Biblical Antiquities, Part II., chap. 8, page 404.

24. What did he further say to them?
Why did not the Nazarenes accept him, or think much of him? —Matt. xiii. 55.
Were the Nazarenes excusable in this? (No.)
Could they find fault with his words?—Ver. 22.

25. What did he then say of the days of Elijah?
Where is this related?—1 Kings xvii. 8-24.
What is meant by the heavens being shut up for three years and six months? (There was no rain.)
What is a *famine?* (A scarcity of food.)

26. To whom was Elijah sent at that time?
Was Sarepta a Jewish town? (No.)
For what purpose was he sent to this widow?—1 Kings xvii. 9.

27. What happened in Elisha's time?
Where is the account of the cleansing of Naaman the Syrian? —2 Kings v.
What is the account there given?

28. What is said of the people in the synagogue when they heard these things?
Why were they filled with wrath? (Because Jesus would not perform miracles among them, and taught that God confers blessings on whom he pleases, Jew or Gentile.)

29. What did they do to Jesus?
What was the brow of the hill? (The edge.)
Had Jesus done any thing that deserved this treatment? (No; he had just been teaching them in the synagogue.)

30. How did Jesus get away from them?
How could he do this? (By his divine power.)
How is Christ often rejected *now?*
When you hear the gospel, and read the words of Jesus, are you not as much bound to believe and obey as the Jews were who heard him speak?
What will be done with those who will not hear the gospel?—John xii. 48.

LESSON IV.

The Beginning of Christ's Sermon on the Mount.

MATT. V. 1-16.

1 And seeing the multitudes, he went up into a mountain: and when he was set, his disciples came unto him:
2 And he opened his mouth, and taught them, saying,

3 Blessed *are* the poor in spirit: for theirs is the kingdom of heaven.
4 Blessed *are* they that mourn: for they shall be comforted.

INSTRUCTIONS OF THE SAVIOUR. 15

5 Blessed *are* the meek: for they shall inherit the earth.
6 Blessed *are* they which do hunger and thirst after righteousness: for they shall be filled.
7 Blessed *are* the merciful: for they shall obtain mercy.
8 Blessed *are* the pure in heart: for .hey shall see God.
9 Blessed *are* the peacemakers: for they shall be alled the children of God.
10 Blessed *are* they which are persecuted for righteousness' sake: for theirs is the kingdom of heaven.
11 Blessed are ye, when *men* shall revile you, and persecute *you*, and shall say all manner of evil against you falsely, for my sake.
12 Rejoice, and be exceeding glad: for great *is* your reward in heaven: for so persecuted they the prophets which were before you.
13 ¶ Ye are the salt of the earth: but if the salt have lost his savour, wherewith shall it be salted? it is thenceforth good for nothing, but to be cast out, and to be trodden under foot of men.
14 Ye are the light of the world. A city that is set on a hill cannot be hid.
15 Neither do men light a candle, and put it under a bushel, but on a candlestick; and it giveth light unto all that are in the house.
16 Let your light so shine before men, that they may see your good works, and glorify your Father which is in heaven.

1. WHEN Jesus saw the multitudes, where did he go?
What multitudes were these?—Matt. iv. 25.
What is this discourse commonly called from its being delivered on a mountain? (The Sermon on the Mount.)
Where else is part of it found?—Luke vi. 20–49.
Who were the disciples of Jesus? (His attendants and followers.)

2. What is said of Jesus after his disciples came to him?

3. Whom did Christ first declare blessed?
What is meant by blessed? (Happy.)
Who are the *poor in spirit?* (The humble; the penitent; those who submit patiently to the will of God.)
Why should men be humble?—Job xiv. 1–4.
Have they any cause to be proud?—1 Cor. iv. 7; Rom. iii. 23; Job viii. 9.
What other promises has God given to the poor in spirit?—Ps. cxxxviii. 6; Isa. lvii. 15.
How is this blessing mentioned by Luke?—Luke vi. 20.
How can it be a blessing to be poor? (Because patient poverty often leads to heavenly riches.)
Do you remember any of the promises and consolations that the Bible gives to the poor?—Ps. cxlvi. 7–9; Prov. xv. 16.
But is it meant that God will bless every one who is poor, whether they love him or not?—Isaiah lxvi. 2; James ii. 5.
Are those who are poor in money and goods always poor in spirit? (No.)
How can you become poor in spir't?—Matt. xi. 29.

4. Whom did Jesus next speak of?
What is meant by mourning? (Sorrowing for sin.)
Why is it blessed to mourn for sin?—Psalm xxxiv. 18.
Why are Christians blessed when they mourn in affliction?—Job v. 17, 18.

What does the apostle Paul say of the difference between the sorrow of Christians and of others?—2 Cor. vii. 10.

5. What did Christ say about the meek?
What is it to be meek? (To be gentle, patient, and kind.)
Who is spoken of in the Old Testament as very meek?—Num. xii. 3.
Do you remember any instances in which he showed his meekness?—Ex. xvi. 2-8.
Who is the greatest model of meekness? (Jesus Christ.)
What is said of his meekness?—1 Pet. ii. 22, 23.
What is promised to the meek?
What is probably meant by that? (Literally, their days shall be longer; sin shortens life: they shall be as contented with what God has given them as though the earth was theirs.)
Where is the same expression found?—Ps. xxxvii. 11.
How did the Jews understand such a promise? (They thought it applied to the land of Canaan.)
Can you mention some of the advantages of being meek? (It produces peace, love, kindness, and patience under injuries and afflictions.)

6. Who are next said to be blessed?
What is it to hunger and thirst after righteousness? (To desire it earnestly.)
Why should we feel such strong desires for righteousness?—Matt. xxv. 46.
How did Job value the words of God?—Job xxiii. 12.
How did David express his feelings towards God?—Ps. xlii. 1, 2.
What is promised to such?
What does that mean? (Their desires shall be gratified by their becoming, through faith, righteous in the sight of God.)
How are they *filled* in this life?—Rom. xv. 13.
How will they be filled hereafter?—Ps. xvii. 15.
What is the invitation of the Bible now?—Isa. lv. 1, 2; Rev. xxii. 17.

7. Whom did Christ next declare to be blessed?
Who are merciful men? (Those who are kind and compassionate.)
To whom should we show mercy? (To all who are in affliction or trouble.)
Do you remember the parable of the good Samaritan?—Luke x. 30–37.
Why should men be merciful?—1 John iii. 17; Micah vi. 8.
What is promised to the merciful?
From whom will they obtain mercy? (From God.)—Ex. xxxiv. 6.
What motive must men have in doing good, if they are thus blessed?—See Mark ix. 41.
Do you remember the parable of the two servants?—Matt. xviii. 23–35.

INSTRUCTIONS OF THE SAVIOUR. 17

8. To whom is the blessing here given?
What is it to be *pure in heart?* (To have the thoughts and motives pure.)
Is the heart of any one pure by nature?—1 Kings viii. 46.
How may the heart become pure?—1 Peter i. 22, 23.
May not a person be pure in his conduct, and yet not pure in heart?—Mark x. 17-22.
Can he be pure in heart and not pure in conduct?—Luke vi. 43-45.
What is the blessing of the poor in heart?
What is meant by their *seeing God?* (They shall receive his favour here, and be admitted to his presence in heaven.)
When will they see God?—Job xix. 25, 26.
What does the apostle John say of this?—1 John iii. 2, 3.

9. Who are next mentioned?
What is a peacemaker? (One who seeks to promote peace.)
Why is this a lovely character? (It is like the Prince of peace.)
Why should men live peaceably together?—Heb. xii. 14, 15.
How can we make peace? (We can often do it by our influence, example, and advice.)
What is commanded to Christians especially?—Eph. iv. 31, 32.
What is the blessing of the peacemakers?
What is it to be the children of God?—Rom. viii. 14.
What is God sometimes called in the Scriptures?—Rom. xv. 33.
What exhortation does the apostle give from this?—2 Cor. xiii. 11.

10. Who are said in this verse to be blessed?
What is it to be persecuted for righteousness' sake? (To suffer injurious treatment for obedience to God's commands.)
What is said to be theirs?
What is meant by the kingdom of heaven? (The grace of God here and hereafter heaven.)

11. What is said in this verse?
What is it to *revile?* (To say hard and abusive things.)
May not evil things be said *truly* of some people? (Yes.)
Is the blessing pronounced upon such?
Is the blessing promised to those who act foolishly and imprudently, and try to get reproaches? (No; such conduct is wrong.)
To whom alone does it apply?—1 Peter ii. 19, 20.

12. How does Jesus encourage such?
Who had suffered the same treatment?
Who are meant by the *prophets?* (Those who had been sent to predict future events.)
Who persecuted the prophets? (The Jews.)—Luke xiii. 34.
Can you mention any in particular who were persecuted for speaking the truth?—1 Kings xix. 13, 14; 2 Chron. xxiv. 20, 21; Jer. xx. 2, and xxxviii. 6.

What did the Lord Jesus himself suffer from persecution? (He was persecuted through all his life, and even unto death.)
Why are wicked and worldly men so angry at those who tell them the truth?—John iii. 19, 20.
How should you behave towards those who tell you of your sins?
How should we act towards those who oppose the truth?—2 Tim. ii. 25.

13. What does Jesus call his disciples?
What is the use of salt? (To preserve and season food.)
Why are God's people said to be the salt of the earth? (Their influence is to the world what salt is to food,—preserving and purifying.)
How must they live if they would have this character?—Rom. xii. 2.
If Christians are like the rest of the world in their practices, can they be said to be the salt of the earth? (No.)
What did Christ say of salt that has lost its savour?
What is the meaning of *savour?* (The quality which makes it valuable.)
How is this said in Mark's Gospel?—Mark ix. 50.
When are Christians like salt that has no savour?—Rev. iii. 2.
What is done with such salt?
How does this apply to inconsistent Christians?—Heb. vi. 4–8.
How may young Christians so live as to be the salt of the earth?—John xv. 4.

14. What does Jesus here call his disciples?
What is the use of light?—Eph. v. 13.
How are Christ's people the light of the world?—Phil. ii. 15.
From whom do they receive their light? (From our Lord Jesus Christ.)
How should they show this light? (By a holy life.)
What did Christ call himself?—John viii. 12.
What else did he compare his disciples to?
How are they like a city on a hill? (Their belief, profession, and example make them conspicuous?)
Is not the conduct of a Christian noticed by other persons?—2 Cor. iii. 2.
If *he* commits sins, what great injury does it do? (It brings reproach upon the religion he professes.)

15. What did Christ say is the use of light?
What is meant by this comparison? (Christians should live to benefit those around them.)

16. What then is the duty of Christ's disciples?
How can they let their light shine?—Titus ii. 12–14.
What would men see?
For what purpose should this be done?

INSTRUCTIONS OF THE SAVIOUR. 19

How are men lead to glorify God by seeing the good example of Christians? (They are won by it to follow Christ themselves.)

What is the difference between this command of Christ and that in Matt. vi. 1? (They both teach that the motive of every right action must be the glory of God and not the praise of men.)

LESSON V.

Christ came not to destroy the Law—he teaches that it extends to the thoughts.

WHAT part of the Scriptures was the subject of the last lesson? Why is it called the sermon on the mount?

MATTHEW V. 17—30.

17 ¶ Think not that I am come to destroy the law, or the prophets: I am not come to destroy, but to fulfil.

18 For verily I say unto you, Till heaven and earth pass, one jot or one tittle shall in no wise pass from the law, till all be fulfilled.

19 Whosoever therefore shall break one of these least commandments, and shall teach men so, he shall be called the least in the kingdom of heaven: but whosoever shall do and teach *them*, the same shall be called great in the kingdom of heaven.

20 For I say unto you, That except your righteousness shall exceed *the righteousness* of the scribes and Pharisees, ye shall in no case enter into the kingdom of heaven.

21 ¶ Ye have heard that it was said by them of old time, Thou shalt not kill; and whosoever shall kill shall be in danger of the judgment:

22 But I say unto you, That whosoever is angry with his brother without a cause shall be in danger of the judgment: and whosoever shall say to his brother, Raca, shall be in danger of the council: but whosoever shall say, Thou fool, shall be in danger of hell fire.

23 Therefore if thou bring thy gift to the altar, and there rememberest that thy brother hath aught against thee:

24 Leave there thy gift before the altar, and go thy way; first be reconciled to thy brother, and then come and offer thy gift.

25 Agree with thine adversary quickly, whiles thou art in the way with him; lest at any time the adversary deliver thee to the judge, and the judge deliver thee to the officer, and thou be cast into prison.

26 Verily I say unto thee, Thou shalt by no means come out thence, till thou hast paid the uttermost farthing.

27 ¶ Ye have heard that it was said by them of old time, Thou shalt not commit adultery:

28 But I say unto you, That whosoever looketh on a woman to lust after her hath committed adultery with her already in his heart.

29 And if thy right eye offend thee, pluck it out, and cast *it* from thee; for it is profitable for thee that one of thy members should perish, and not *that* thy whole body should be cast into hell.

30 And if thy right hand offend thee, cut if off, and cast *it* from thee: for it is profitable for thee that one of thy members should perish, and not *that* thy whole body should be cast into hell.

17. What did our Lord say he had not come to destroy?

What did he mean by the law and the prophets? (The Old Testament Scriptures.)
What did he mean by saying he did not come to destroy them? (He did not come to repeal them.)
What then did he come to do?
How did Christ fulfil the law? (By obeying it in his life and suffering its penalty in his death.)
How did he fulfil the prophets? (By accomplishing all the prophecies respecting himself.)

18. What does Jesus say of the law in this verse?
What did he mean by saying *till heaven and earth pass?*—See 2 Pet. iii. 10.
What is meant by a *jot* or *tittle?* (Jot is the smallest letter; tittle, a point used in writing: the expression means the least part.)
What part of the law of Moses has been fulfilled and passed away.—See Heb. ix. 10; x. 1.
What part of the law will always be in force?—(The moral law.)
Has any one obeyed this perfectly?—Eccles. vii. 20.
How then can any sinner be saved?—Gal. iii. 13.

19. Who did Jesus say should be called least in the kingdom of heaven?
Are any of God's commandments of small importance?—Gal. iii. 10.
When you break God's laws, and set a bad example before others, do you not *teach* them to sin?
Who shall be called *great* in the kingdom of heaven?
Is it enough to *teach* the commandments of God?
What is the duty of those who *do* the commandments?
How can you teach them?

20. What did Jesus say respecting their righteousness?
What did he mean by their righteousness? (Their purity of heart and life.)
What is the meaning of *exceed?* (To go beyond.)
What was the character of the scribes and Pharisees?—Matt. xxiii. 27, 28.
What does Jesus say of those whose righteousness does not exceed that of the scribes and Pharisees?
What then is true righteousness?—Rom. ii. 29.
What will become of those who are not fit for the kingdom of heaven? Matt. xxv. 41.

21. What had been said of them of old time?
Which of the ten commandments is this?—(The sixth.)
Where do you find it written in the Old Testament?—Ex. xx. 13.
What is the meaning of this commandment? (It forbids taking away life unlawfully.)

INSTRUCTIONS OF THE SAVIOUR. 21

What is the *judgment* here spoken of?*

22. Who did Christ tell them should also be in danger of the judgment?
By what right did he speak these words, "*I* say unto you"? (The right of his Divinity.)—John i. 1.
What connection has anger with the crime of murder? (It is that feeling of the heart which leads to the act of murder.)
What does the apostle John say of this?—1 John iii. 15.
Who is meant by a *brother* here? (A fellow being.)
Why are all men our brethren?—Mal. ii. 10.
How then should we act to all?—Lev. xix. 18.
What did anger lead Cain to do?—1 John iii. 12.
When Joseph's brethren indulged hatred against him, what were they tempted to do?—Gen. xxxvii. 18-21.
Who did Jesus say should be in danger of the council?
What is the meaning of *Raca?* (Worthless.)
What was the council? (Their highest court, the Sanhedrim.)
What was the highest punishment the council could inflict? (They could sentence to death, but in the time of our Saviour the power of executing the sentence had been taken from them by the Romans.)
What does this teach us of the sinfulness of abusive language? —James iv. 11.
Who did the Lord say should be in danger of hell fire?
Can you tell what the word *fool* means here? (A wicked person.)
What is the difference between *Raca* and *fool?* (Raca expresses contempt, fool is an accusation of crime.)
What did Christ probably mean by what is here called *hell fire?* (The fires in the valley of Hinnom, which were so awful as to be a fit image of hell.)
How does Solomon caution us against anger?—Eccl. vii. 9.
If you have any thing against your friend or neighbour, what ought you to do?—Luke xvii. 3, 4.
What is written in Rom. xiv. 19?

23, 24. What is written in these verses?
What was meant by bringing his gift to the altar? (Worshipping God.)
What is the meaning of *reconciled?* (Having kind feeling restored.)
What did the Lord teach by these two verses? (That we cannot worship God while we feel enmity to each other.)
Will God accept the worship of a person who indulges evil feelings towards his fellow-men?—Psalm lxvi. 18.
What did Christ say about this?—Matt. vi. 15.

25. What directions did Jesus give his disciples concerning their adversaries?

---

* See Biblical Antiquities, Part I, ch. 9, sec. 3.

What is an adversary? (An opponent.)
What is meant by their agreeing whilst they were in the way with him? (On their way to the court, quickly.)
Why were they to agree *quickly* with him?
What is the duty of Christians as written in Rom. xii. 18.
How do children often sin in this way?
How should they act if any one has offended them?
How should they act when they have offended others?

26. What is said in this verse?
How is this related in Luke?—Luke xii. 58, 59.
Would it not be better to agree with an adversary than to suffer this?

27. Of what other commandment did Jesus here remind them?
Which commandment is this? (The seventh.)
Where is it written?—Ex. xx. 15.

28. How did Jesus explain this commandment?
Are unholy thoughts then sinful?—Matt. xv. 19, 20.

29. What next did Jesus say?
What is the meaning of *offended* here? (To cause to fall into sin.)
What is meant by *plucking it out?*—And see Gal. v. 24.
Why should this be done?
Then if any thing which is dear to you leads you into sin, what must you do?
Why should you give up those sins which most easily beset you?—Rom. vi. 16.

30. How did Jesus again express this?
What does this teach? (That no evil is so grievous as sin.)

LESSON VI.

Our Lord forbids swearing; teaches his people patiently to endure injuries, to love their enemies, and do good to all.

MATTHEW v. 33–48.

33 ¶ Again, ye have heard that it hath been said by them of old time, Thou shalt not forswear thyself, but shalt perform unto the Lord thine oaths:

34 But I say unto you, Swear not at all; neither by heaven; for it is God's throne:

35 Nor by the earth; for it is his foot-stool: neither by Jerusalem: for it is the city of the great King.

36 Neither shalt thou swear by thy head, because thou canst not make one hair white or black.

37 But let your communication be, Yea, yea; Nay, nay: for whatsoever is more than these cometh of evil.

38 ¶ Ye have heard that it hath been

INSTRUCTIONS OF THE SAVIOUR. 23

said, An eye for an eye, and a tooth for a tooth:
39 But I say unto you, That ye resist not evil: but whosoever shall smite thee on thy right cheek, turn to him the other also.
40 And if any man will sue thee at the law, and take away thy coat, let him have *thy* cloak also.
41 And whosoever shall compel thee to go a mile, go with him twain.
42 Give to him that asketh thee, and from him that would borrow of thee turn not thou away.
43 ¶ Ye have heard that it hath been said, Thou shalt love thy neighbour, and hate thine enemy.
44 But I say unto you, Love your enemies, bless them that curse you, do good to them that hate you, and pray for them which despitefully use you, and persecute you;
45 That ye may be the children of your Father which is in heaven: for he maketh his sun to rise on the evil and on the good, and sendeth rain on the just and on the unjust.
46 For if ye love them which love you, what reward have ye? do not even the publicans the same?
47 And if ye salute your brethren only, what do ye more *than others?* do not even the publicans so?
48 Be ye therefore perfect, even as your Father which is in heaven is perfect.

33. WHAT is said in this verse of the sermon on the mount?
What was the Jewish law about swearing?
Where is this written?—Lev. xix. 12.
What is it to forswear one's self? (To take a false oath.)
What are *oaths?* (An oath is a solemn declaration, with an appeal to God for its truth.)
What is meant by *performing* an oath? (Performing faithfully what is promised in the oath.)
Which of the ten commandments relates to swearing? (The third.)
Repeat it as in Ex. xx. 7.

34. What did our Lord say about swearing?
What is it to *swear?* (To take an oath.)
Why may you not swear by heaven?
What do you read in Matt. xxiii. 22?

35. Why are you forbidden to swear by the earth?
Why might not a person swear by Jerusalem?
Where was the city of Jerusalem? (In the southeastern part of Palestine.)
Who is meant by the *great King?*—Ps. xcv. 3.

36. What are you forbidden to swear by in this verse?
What reason is given?
Were such oaths as these that have been mentioned common among profane people? (Yes.)
What is generally the character of the persons who swear?—Ps. cxxxix. 20.
Can any excuse be made for profane swearing? (There can never be any excuse for disobeying God.)
Has God declared any thing about punishing it?—Ex. xx. 7.

37. What did he tell them about their communication?

What is meant by *communication* here ? (Talking.)
What is meant by your communication being Yea, yea, and Nay, nay? (We should simply affirm or deny a thing, and be careful not to use any irreverent expressions.)
Why should it be so?
Where is this repeated?—James v. 12.

38. What else had they heard said?
Was not this part of the law?—Ex. xxi. 24.
What was meant by it? (It was a rule to guide judicial decisions.)

39. What did Christ say?
What is meant by not resisting evil? (To be patient and gentle, and not to retaliate.)
What is written concerning this in Rom xii. 17-19?
What further directions does Jesus give in this verse?
What is the meaning of *smite?* (To strike.)
What is the common practice of men when they are struck?
How does Solomon caution us against the beginning of strife?—Prov. xvii. 14.
What was the example of the Lord Jesus himself?—1 Peter ii. 23.
What do you read in Eph. iv. 31, 32?

40. How else should we show a meek disposition?
Do you know what parts of dress worn by the people of that time are meant by *coat* and *cloak?**
How does the apostle Paul speak to the Corinthian Christians about going to law?—1 Cor. vi. 7.

41. What is the next case mentioned by the Lord?
What is the meaning of *twain?* (Two.)
What is the spirit recommended in this precept?—Rom. xii.18.
May not these precepts of the Lord be obeyed, and yet men preserve their proper rights? (Yes.)

42. How should we show kindness to our fellow-men?
Who freely gives us all that we have?—James i. 17.
For what purpose does he give it?—Isa. xliii. 21. 2 Cor. ix. 10, 11.
What command respecting this did God give to the Jews?—Deut. xv. 7, 8.
What should lead Christians to be liberal?—2 Cor. viii. 9.

43. What had the Jews said about the way of treating their enemies?
Which part of this saying is in the law of God?—See Lev. xix. 18.
Which part had the Jews added? (The last.)
Who is here meant by *thy neighbour?* (Our fellow-beings.)

---

* See Biblical Antiquities, Part I., chap. 5, sec. 1.

INSTRUCTIONS OF THE SAVIOUR.

Whom alone did the Jews consider as their neighbours? (Those who were their friends, and of their nation.)

44. How did Jesus say men should act?
What is an enemy? (One who tries to injure us.)
How must we treat those that abuse us?
What should we do for them?
Why should we treat them in this manner?—Verse 45.
What great reason have we to pray for persons who curse, and hate, and persecute us? (The example of our Saviour.)
What examples of this are in the gospel?—Luke xxiii. 34. Acts vii. 59, 60.

45. Whom would they be like if they acted in this manner?
What is meant by their being children of God? (In loving their enemies they resembled God.)
How does the Lord act towards all?
How is this expressed in the gospel by Luke?—Luke vi. 35.
When will the Lord make a difference in his treatment of the good and the evil?—John v. 23, 29.

46. What question does Jesus ask in this verse?
Who did as much as that?
Who were the *publicans?* (Collectors of the Roman revenue.)
Whom are you bound to love besides those that love you?
Why?

47. What question is asked in this verse?
What is meant by *saluting your brethren?* (Expressing kind wishes.)
Are not even ungodly men often kind to their relations and friends. (Yes.)
Why is a follower of Christ bound to do more than others?—1 Cor. vi. 19, 20.

48. What does Jesus here command his disciples?
Whom does he set before them for an example of perfection?
What is meant here by being *perfect?* (To sincerely take God's perfect law for our rule, and his perfect love for our example.)
Whom alone is it safe to follow and imitate?—1 Peter ii. 21.
In what respect should your behaviour be like that of the Lord Jesus?
Have you any excuse for not having this character?

LESSON VII.

Our Lord teaches how we should perform almsgiving, prayer, and fasting.

MATT. vi. 1-10.

1 Take heed that ye do not your alms before men, to be seen of them: otherwise ye have no reward of your Father which is in heaven.
2 Therefore when thou doest *thine* alms, do not sound a trumpet before thee, as the hypocrites do in the synagogues and in the streets, that they may have glory of men. Verily I say unto you, They have their reward.
3 But when thou doest alms, let not thy left hand know what thy right hand doeth:
4 That thine alms may be in secret: and thy Father which seeth in secret himself shall reward thee openly.
5 ¶ And when thou prayest, thou shalt not be as the hypocrites *are:* for they love to pray standing in the synagogues and in the corners of the streets, that they may be seen of men.
Verily I say unto you, They have their reward.
6 But thou, when thou prayest, enter into thy closet, and when thou hast shut thy door, pray to thy Father which is in secret; and thy Father which seeth in secret shall reward thee openly.
7 But when ye pray, use not vain repetitions, as the heathen *do:* for they think that they shall be heard for their much speaking.
8 Be not ye therefore like unto them: for your Father knoweth what things ye have need of, before ye ask him.
9 After this manner therefore pray ye: Our Father which art in heaven, Hallowed be thy name.
10 Thy kingdom come. Thy will be done in earth, as *it is* in heaven.

1. WHAT is meant by doing *alms?* (Giving to the poor.)
What rule did our Lord give about giving alms?
What is meant by doing alms *to be seen* of men? (Seeking the praise of men in doing them.)
Should a Christian never let his good works be known? (Yes, if the motive be right, it does not matter whether the action be public or private.)
Why should a Christian let men see the good he does?—Matt. v. 16.
How then do these two rules agree? (They show us that the glory of God should be our aim in every thing we do.)
What does Jesus say to those who do good for the sake of being seen?
What should be our chief design in giving alms and doing good works?—Heb. xiii. 16.
What reward shall be given to those who do their alms from a right motive?—Matt. xxv. 34-40.

2. What must be avoided in giving alms?
What is a *hypocrite?* (One who pretends to be what he is not.)
What is meant by their sounding a trumpet before them? (Trying to attract attention.)
Why did they sound a trumpet?
What is said of the Pharisees in John xii. 43?

INSTRUCTIONS OF THE SAVIOUR. 27

Do hypocrites get what they seek for?
What *is* their reward? (What they seek, the praise of men.)

3. How should alms be given?
What does that mean? (It should be done without ostentation.)

4. Why should it be done in this manner?
When shall such be rewarded openly?—Luke xiv. 13, 14.

5. In what other duty does Jesus warn his people not to be as the hypocrites?
How did the hypocrites love to pray?
Why did they stand in such conspicuous places?
Why did they wish to be seen of men? (To gain a reputation for piety.)
What shall hypocrites receive?

6. What directions does Jesus here give respecting prayer?
What is here meant by a *closet?* (A retired place.)
Why should we pray alone? (Because we need God's blessing individually.)
What is the advantage of praying alone? (We can pray without reserve.)
Why is it called *secret* prayer? (It is not under the observation of others.)
What promise is given to those that pray in this manner?
Is it not right for people to meet together and worship God in public?—Heb. x. 25.
Where do we read in the New Testament of Christians meeting together for prayer?—Acts i. 14; xii. 12.

7. What other direction did the Lord give about prayer?
What are vain repetitions? (Words repeated in an unmeaning or thoughtless manner.)
What kind of people did so?
Who are here meant by the heathen? (The Gentiles.)
Is it wrong to repeat the same words in prayer, or to ask many times for the same thing? (No.)
How is our Lord's meaning explained in the rest of the verse? (We are not to repeat as though God did not hear.)
Why did the heathen use repetitions?
How did the Lord speak of the prayers of the Pharisees?—Matt. xv. 8.
Will your prayers be acceptable if your heart is not engaged?

8. Why should we not be like these heathen?

Why then is it right and necessary to pray? (God's blessing is promised to those who ask it.)
What do you read of the example of Jesus?—See Mark i. 35; Luke vi. 12.

9. What does Jesus teach his disciples in this verse?
Why is this commonly called *the Lord's Prayer?* (Because it was given by our Lord to his disciples.)
What is meant by *after this manner?* (Like this.)
Must all our prayers be exactly in these words? (No.)
How then must it be followed? (As a guide how to pray and what to pray for.)
What does he teach them to call God?
How is God the Father of all? (He is their Creator, Benefactor, and Preserver.)
How is he especially the father of Christians?—Rom. viii. 14, 15.
Where is God said to be?
How is God said to be in heaven, when we are told that he is everywhere present?—Isa. lxvi. 1.
What are we taught to pray respecting God's name?
What is the meaning of *hallowed?* (To be revered and esteemed as holy.)
How is the name of the Lord to be hallowed?—Ps. lxxxvi. 9-12.

10. What are we taught to pray respecting God's kingdom?
What is meant here by God's *kingdom?* (His reign.)
What do you mean by praying for this kingdom to *come?*—(That it may be advanced everywhere.)
Is God known and obeyed as the King of all the earth? (No.)
How do men show that they do not wish God to reign over them?—Jer. vii. 23, 24.
How is it seen in pagan countries that the kingdom of God has not come among them?—Kings xxi. 26.
What can men do to extend his kingdom?—Matt. xxviii. 19.
What is written respecting the time when the Lord shall be King over the whole world?—Zech. xiv. 9; Rev. xi. 15.
What are you taught to pray respecting the will of God?
What is meant by *the will* of God? (His law.)
Whose will do most people desire to have done? (Their own.)
What would be the consequence if God's will were done by all? (We should be happy like the angels.)
How is the will of God done in heaven, and by whom?—Ps. ciii. 20, 21.
How can you know what is the will of God?—2 Tim. iii. 16, 17.
Is it enough to know his will?—John xiii. 17.
What did Jesus say of those who do the will of God?—Matt. xii. 50.
What of those who do not the will of God?—Luke xii. 47

LESSON VIII.

The Lord's Prayer, continued.

MATT. vi. 11-18.

11 Give us this day our daily bread.
12 And forgive us our debts, as we forgive our debtors.
13 And lead us not into temptation, but deliver us from evil: For thine is the kingdom, and the power, and the glory, for ever. Amen.
14 For if ye forgive men their trespasses, your heavenly Father will also forgive you:
15 But if ye forgive not men their trespasses, neither will your Father forgive your trespasses.

16 ¶ Moreover when ye fast, be not, as the hypocrites, of a sad countenance: for they disfigure their faces, that they may appear unto men to fast. Verily I say unto you, They have their reward.
17 But thou, when thou fastest, anoint thine head, and wash thy face;
18 That thou appear not unto men to fast, but unto thy Father which is in secret: and thy Father which seeth in secret shall reward thee openly.

11. WHAT is the next thing we are taught to pray for?
How is this written by Luke?—Luke xi. 3.
What is meant by *bread* here? (That which is needful to sustain life.)
What is *daily* bread? (The supply of each day's wants.)
Why are people taught to ask their bread of God, when they must earn it themselves? (They cannot earn it without his blessing on their efforts.—Eccles. iii. 13.)
Why ought you daily to thank God for food?—Ps. cxxxvi. 25, 26.

12. What is the next subject mentioned?
What are meant here by *debts?* (Sins.)
Who are meant here by *debtors?* (Those who have injured us.)
How is this expressed by Luke?—Luke xi. 4.
What is it to *forgive a debt?* (To forgive an injury.)
What do you owe to God for all his goodness to you?—Deut. xi. 1; Ps. cxvi. 12-14.
Have you ever paid this debt?
How does God forgive the debts or sins of his people?—Col. i. 13, 14.
If you do not from your heart forgive those who have offended you, can you expect God will forgive you?—Verse 15.
Who has set you a good example in the forgiveness of injuries? Luke xxiii. 34.
If your sins against God are not forgiven, what must become of you?
Can you give some account of the parable written in Matt. xviii. 21-35.

13. What does Jesus teach us to pray respecting temptation?
What is *temptation?* (Enticement to evil.)
Does God ever tempt people to sin?—James i. 13-15.

What then is meant by this prayer? (That God would keep us from being tempted to sin.)
Why should God's people pray not to be led into temptation? (Unless God helps them they cannot withstand it.)
If they be led into temptation, or placed in trying circumstances, what promise have they?—1 Cor. x. 13.
Does this promise belong to those who run into temptation? (No.)
What is promised to those who endure temptation without sinning?—James i. 12.
How are the young exposed to temptation?
Ought you not to avoid such circumstances, and company, and employments as are calculated to lead you into temptation?
If you use this prayer, what ought you to do with regard to these things?—Prov. iv. 14, 15, 26, 27.

From what does Jesus teach us to pray to be delivered?
What is meant here by *evil?* (All sin and misery.)
What is it to be *delivered* from evil? (To be released from it.)
What are the evils to which we are exposed in this life? (Our own evil hearts, temporal sufferings, and the snares of Satan.)
What is the greatest evil in the world? (Sin.)—Jer. ii. 19.
What did Jesus ask for his people?—John xvii. 15.
For whose sake will God deliver his people from evil?—Rom. v. 10.

What is the reason why we should offer these petitions to God?
How is the *kingdom* his? (He controls and governs all things.—Ps. xxii. 28.)
What is meant by the *power* that is ascribed to God?—Dan. iv. 35.
Why does all the *glory* belong to God?—Ex. xv. 11.

How long will the kingdom, and the power, and the glory be the Lord's?
What is written in Rev. v. 11-14?

What is the last word of this prayer?
What is the meaning of *Amen?* (So let it be.)
Should this be said thoughtlessly? (No.)

14. What did our Lord say about the necessity of our forgiving others?
What part of the Lord's prayer does this refer to? (The fifth petition.)
What do you mean by *trespasses?* (Offences, injuries.)
What is meant by *forgiving* them? (Feeling and acting just as kindly as before the offence.)

15. What if you do not forgive?

16. What caution does our Lord give about fasting?
What is it to *fast?* (To abstain from food.)

How did the hypocrites fast?
What is meant by their disfiguring their faces? (They neglected their hair, threw ashes on their heads, and assumed a gloomy expression of face.)
What is said about fasts in Isa. lviii. 5-7.
Is any service acceptable to God if men are not sincere?—Matt. xv. 7-9.
Why not?—Ps. xliv. 21.

17. How should the Christian fast?
What is the meaning of this? (They should let their outward appearance be as usual.)

18. Why should this be done?
Does God regard the outward appearance?—1 Sam. xvi. 7.
Why should we not wish to appear to men to fast? (If we do it to attract notice it is hypocrisy.)
Against what does our Lord guard his people in all these directions? (Against insincerity and ostentation.)

LESSON IX.

The Sermon on the Mount, continued.

MATT. vi. 19-34.

19 ¶ Lay not up for yourselves treasures upon earth, where moth and rust doth corrupt, and where thieves break through and steal:
20 But lay up for yourselves treasures in heaven, where neither moth nor rust doth corrupt, and where thieves do not break through nor steal:
21 For where your treasure is, there will your heart be also.
22 The light of the body is the eye: if therefore thine eye be single, thy whole body shall be full of light.
23 But if thine eye be evil, thy whole body shall be full of darkness. If therefore the light that is in thee be darkness, how great is that darkness!
24 ¶ No man can serve two masters: for either he will hate the one, and love the other; or else he will hold to the one, and despise the other. Ye cannot serve God and mammon.
25 Therefore I say unto you, Take no thought for your life, what ye shall eat, or what ye shall drink; nor yet for your body, what ye shall put on. Is not the life more than meat, and the body than raiment?

26 Behold the fowls of the air: for they sow not, neither do they reap, nor gather into barns; yet your heavenly Father feedeth them. Are ye not much better than they?
27 Which of you by taking thought can add one cubit unto his stature?
28 And why take ye thought for raiment? Consider the lilies of the field, how they grow; they toil not, neither do they spin?
29 And yet I say unto you, That even Solomon in all his glory was not arrayed like one of these.
30 Wherefore, if God so clothe the grass of the field, which to-day is, and to-morrow is cast into the oven, *shall he* not much more *clothe* you, O ye of little faith?
31 Therefore take no thought, saying, What shall we eat? or, What shall we drink? or, Wherewithal shall we be clothed?
32 (For after all these things do the Gentiles seek:) for your heavenly Father knoweth that ye have need of all these things.
33 But seek ye first the kingdom of

God, and his righteousness; and all these things shall be added unto you. 34 Take therefore no thought for the morrow: for the morrow shall take thought for the things of itself. Sufficient unto the day is the evil thereof.

19. WHAT is the next subject of our Lord's instructions?
What is the meaning of *treasures?* (Something valued.)
What is meant by laying up treasures on earth? (Seeking worldly possessions.)
Why should we not do it?
What is a *moth?* (An insect which eats clothing.)
What is *rust?* (That which destroys metals.)
How are earthly treasures liable to these accidents?
What shall be the end of all earthly treasures?—2 Peter iii. 10.
What often becomes of riches even whilst their owners are alive?—Prov. xxiii. 5.
When will they certainly leave them?—See 1 Tim. vi. 7.

20. Where should we lay up treasures?
What is meant by laying up treasures in heaven?
How may this be done?—Acts xvi. 31.
Will that treasure last?
How is it then foolish as well as sinful to desire earthly riches above every thing else?—Luke xii. 16-21.
Is not the soul as capable of happiness as the body?—Ps. xxxv. 9.
Will riches satisfy the soul?—Ezek. vii. 19.
What does Jesus say to those who look for treasure above?—John xiv. 1-3.
What do you read about them in Rev. vii. 14-17?

21. Where will your heart be?
How do explain that? (What we think most about, and love most, is our treasure.)
What do you read about a certain ruler to whom Jesus offered treasure in heaven?—Luke xviii. 18-24.
Where should your heart and affections be?—Col. iii. 1, 2.
If riches are given to us, how should we employ them?—1 Tim. vi. 17, 18.

22. What is the eye said to be?
What is meant by that? (Light enters the eye.)
When shall "the whole body be full of light"?
What is meant by the eye being *single?* (Seeing clearly.)
What is meant by the whole body being full of light? (Being influenced by the light.)

23. What if the eye be *evil?*
What is meant by the eye being evil? (Diseased or injured.)
How does Jesus apply this?
What is meant by the light that is in men? (Their mind and conscience.)

INSTRUCTIONS OF THE SAVIOUR. 33

What makes the minds of men dark and blind, that they choose *earthly* rather than heavenly things?—2 Cor. iv. 4.
How is spiritual light given to the mind?—Ps. cxix. 130.
Why are sinners said to be blind?—Eph. iv. 18.
How does the desire of riches blind the mind?—1 Tim. vi. 9, 10.

24. What more did Christ say?
Why can he not do it?
What two masters does Jesus say you cannot serve together?
What is meant by *mammon?* (Earthly riches.)
What is it to serve mammon? (To make gaining riches our chief aim.)
What is it to serve God?—Ps. xxxvii. 3.
What is written in 1 John ii. 15-17?
How may we know whether we are servants of God or mammon?—Rom. vi. 16.
Whom is it our duty to serve?—Luke iv. 8.
How should we do it?—1 Chron. xxviii. 9.

25. What did Jesus therefore say to them?
What is meant by *taking thought* for the life and for the body? (Taking anxious care.)
Does this command require us not to labour nor to provide for our wants? (No.)
How do you know this is not meant?—See 1 Tim. v. 8; 2 Thess. iii. 10.
What does it mean?—Ps. iv. 5; Phil. iv. 6.
What question does Jesus then ask?
Who gave you life, and formed your body?—Job xxxiii. 4.
Cannot he give you meat to preserve your life, and raiment to clothe your body?—Ps. civ. 28.
How is this stated in Luke?—Luke xii. 23.

26. What did the Lord then speak of?
How are they taken care of?
How is this told in Luke?—Luke xii. 24.
But are they not industrious?
What question did he then ask?
In what respect are you better or of more importance than the fowls? (In having an immortal soul.)
What did Jesus mean to teach his people by this? (To trust in God.)

27. What question is asked in this verse?
What is the meaning of *stature?* (Height.)
What is a *cubit?* (About nineteen inches.)
How is this explained?—Luke xii. 26.

28, 29. What did our Lord say about raiment?
What is *raiment?* (Clothing.)

What does he bid them consider?
What is it to *toil?* (To labour.)
What is said of their beauty?
What is the meaning of *arrayed?* (Dressed.)
Is not the same God over all things?—Neh. ix. 6.

30. How did Christ apply this?
What did he mean by saying "the grass to-day is, and to-morrow is cast into the oven"? (It is growing one day, and burned the next.)
Do you know what sort of ovens were used in Judea? (Those most used were excavations in the earth, paved with stones.)
How did he call the people?
How does it show want of faith for Christians to be very anxious about their support in life? (It shows they do not trust the promises of God.)
What did the apostle Paul say that may be applied to this?—Rom. viii. 32.

31. What then did Christ advise?

32. Who were concerned about these things?
Who were Gentiles? (Heathen nations.)
Why should Christians be free from such cares?—Heb. xiii. 5.
What reason does Jesus give them for it here?

33. What should be first sought?
What are meant by the kingdom of God and his righteousness? (His forgiveness and favour.)
How are these to be sought?—Deut. iv. 29.
When should they be sought?—2 Cor. vi. 2.
What is promised to those who shall seek?
All what things? (The supply of our temporal wants.)

34. How did he end this advice?
What is the meaning of that? (Do not be anxious about it.)
What is meant by "sufficient unto the day is the evil thereof"?
(Each day has care enough of its own.)
What effect has too much anxiety concerning our future support upon us?
Why should we not have *great* anxiety about it?—James iv. 14.
How should men feel as to their future life?—Luke xiii. 24.

INSTRUCTIONS OF THE SAVIOUR. 35

LESSON X.

The Sermon on the Mount, continued.

Do you remember what was the principal subject of the last lesson?

MATT. vii. 1–14.

1 Judge not, that ye be not judged.
2 For with what judgment ye judge, ye shall be judged: and with what measure ye mete, it shall be measured to you again.
3 And why beholdest thou the mote that is in thy brother's eye, but considerest not the beam that is in thine own eye?
4 Or how wilt thou say to thy brother, Let me pull out the mote out of thine eye; and, behold, a beam is in thine own eye?
5 Thou hypocrite, first cast out the beam out of thine own eye; and then shalt thou see clearly to cast out the mote out of thy brother's eye.
6 ¶ Give not that which is holy unto the dogs, neither cast ye your pearls before swine, lest they trample them under their feet, and turn again and rend you.
7 ¶ Ask, and it shall be given you; seek, and ye shall find; knock, and it shall be opened unto you:
8 For every one that asketh receiveth; and he that seeketh findeth; and to him that knocketh it shall be opened.
9 Or what man is there of you, whom if his son ask bread, will he give him a stone?
10 Or if he ask a fish, will he give him a serpent?
11 If ye then, being evil, know how to give good gifts unto your children, how much more shall your Father which is in heaven give good things to them that ask him?
12 Therefore all things whatsoever ye would that men should do to you, do ye even so to them: for this is the law and the prophets.
13 ¶ Enter ye in at the strait gate: for wide is the gate, and broad is the way, that leadeth to destruction, and many there be which go in thereat:
14 Because strait is the gate, and narrow is the way, which leadeth unto life, and few there be that find it.

1. WHAT was the next commandment which the Lord gave?
What kind of judging is meant? (Censorious.)
Why have men no right to judge others in this way? (It is always unkind, and often unjust.)
What words of our Lord may be applied to such a case?—John viii. 7.
What reason is given for keeping this rule?
What is meant by that? (We shall receive such judgment as we give.)

2. How shall men be judged?
What is the meaning of the whole of this verse? (The rule by which we judge others will be applied to us.)
If we condemn others for the same sins that we do ourselves, how does that condemn us?—And see Rom. ii. 1, 3, 21.

3. What question does Jesus ask in this verse?
What is a *mote*? (A small particle.)
What is meant by a *beam*? (A large piece of timber.)

How do you explain this? (We are often ignorant of our own great faults (beams), while we see plainly the small faults (motes) of others.
Why should we correct our own faults before we reprove others?

4. What did our Lord ask?
Who is meant by a *brother* here? (A fellow being.)
Explain this. (It shows the inconsistency of censuring others while we are more faulty than they.)

5. What does the Lord call such a man?
How is he a hypocrite? (In pretending to be good.)
What should he first do?
What directions does the Bible give for telling others of their faults, if we do it with a proper spirit?—See Lev. xix. 17. Matt. xviii. 15.
How should it be done?—Gal. vi. 1.

6. What is the next verse?
What does he mean by *pearls* and *that which is holy?* (The doctrines and precepts of the Gospel.)
What sort of people does he mean by dogs and swine? (Wicked and abusive.)
What are we taught by this? (Not to offer these doctrines publicly to those who will abuse them.)

7. What does Jesus bid his disciples do?
What promise is made if they ask?
What should you ask of God?—1 John v. 14.
What promise is made to those who seek?
What is it to seek? (To endeavour to find.)
What are you to seek?—1 Chron. xvi. 11.
What promise is made in Matt. v. 6?
What assurance have those that knock?
What is meant by knocking? (Earnest effort.)
What is written as the voice of wisdom in Prov. viii. 34?

8. What is said about him that asks, seeks, and knocks?
What is meant by this? (That God will answer prayer.)
How is it then that some ask and do not receive?—James iv. 3, and i. 6, 7.
With what spirit should you seek the blessing of God?
Repeat Heb. xi. 6.
What is written of those who put off seeking aright until it is too late?—Luke xiii. 25.
What is said to the young?—Eccl. xii. 1; Prov. viii. 17.
For whose sake do God's people receive any thing at his hands? (For Jesus Christ's sake.)

9, 10. What does Christ refer to in these verses?

INSTRUCTIONS OF THE SAVIOUR.

11. What does Jesus teach from this?
To whom is God ready to give blessings?
What blessing did Christ particularly mention?—See Luke xi. 13.
What excuse then have any for not asking? (Not any.)

12. What rule is given here?
How is it given by another evangelist?—Luke vi. 31.
How do you wish your fellow-creatures to treat you?
How then must you treat them?
What would be the effect on the world if this rule were followed?—Isaiah xxxii. 17, 18.
Would there be murder, or robbery, or slandering, or unkindness?—Rom. xiii. 9, 10.
If we were in poverty and distress, how would we wish others to act to us?
How then should we act to those who are so?
What does Jesus add in this verse?
What is meant by that? (It is a summary of what the Scriptures command.)
How did Christ afterwards speak of this?—Matt. xxii. 35-40.

13. At what does Jesus bid his disciples enter in?
What is meant by the *strait gate?* (The entrance to the Way of Life.)
What is the difference between *strait* and *straight?* (Strait means narrow; straight, not crooked.)
Why is the entrance to Christ's kingdom called *strait?* (It is not natural nor easy to our evil hearts.)
Why should the strait gate be chosen?
Why is this called a *wide* gate and a *broad* way? (It suits and gives license to the evil of our natures.)
What is meant by the *destruction* to which it leads?—2 Thess. i. 9.
Who are those who walk in the broad way to ruin?—Jer. xvi. 12.
Why do they walk in it?—John iii. 19.

14. Why do so many go in the broad way?
To what life does the narrow way lead?—Rom. vi. 23.
How do those conduct themselves who are walking in the narrow way?—Titus ii. 12.
What makes this way so narrow and hard? (Our hearts are naturally averse to that which is good.)
What is that which makes it a way of pleasantness and a path of peace?—Ps xix. 8, 11; Ps. lxxiii. 24.
Why do so few find it?—John v. 40.

LESSON XI.

Conclusion of the Sermon on the Mount.

MATT. vii. 15-29.

15 ¶ Beware of false prophets, which come to you in sheep's clothing, but inwardly they are ravening wolves.
16 Ye shall know them by their fruits. Do men gather grapes of thorns, or figs of thistles?
17 Even so every good tree bringeth forth good fruit; but a corrupt tree bringeth forth evil fruit.
18 A good tree cannot bring forth evil fruit, neither can a corrupt tree bring forth good fruit.
19 Every tree that bringeth not forth good fruit is hewn down, and cast into the fire.
20 Wherefore by their fruits ye shall know them.
21 ¶ Not every one that saith unto me, Lord, Lord, shall enter into the kingdom of heaven; but he that doeth the will of my Father which is in heaven.
22 Many will say to me in that day, Lord, Lord, have we not prophesied in thy name? and in thy name have cast out devils? and in thy name done many wonderful works?
23 And then will I profess unto them, I never knew you: depart from me, ye that work iniquity.
24 ¶ Therefore whosoever heareth these sayings of mine, and doeth them, I will liken him unto a wise man, which built his house upon a rock:
25 And the rain descended, and the floods came, and the winds blew, and beat upon that house; and it fell not: for it was founded upon a rock.
26 And every one that heareth these sayings of mine, and doeth them not, shall be likened unto a foolish man, which built his house upon the sand:
27 And the rain descended, and the floods came, and the winds blew, and beat upon that house; and it fell: and great was the fall of it.
28 And it came to pass, when Jesus had ended these sayings, the people were astonished at his doctrine:
29 For he taught them as one having authority, and not as the scribes.

15. OF whom did Christ tell his hearers to beware?
Who are meant by *false prophets?* (Those who teach religious error.)
What is signified by their being in sheep's clothing? (Having the appearance of piety.)
How did they come?
What did our Lord say they were inwardly?
What did he mean by this? (They were the enemies of religion.)
Are there any false teachers now? (Yes.)
Why should you beware of them? (Because the welfare of our immortal souls depends upon believing exactly what the Word of God teaches.)
What does the apostle Peter say of false teachers?—2 Pet. ii. 1.
What does Paul say to the Galatians?—Gal. i. 8.
What is said on the subject in 2 John 9-11?
By what rule should we judge of the doctrines of any teacher?—Isaiah viii. 20.
How will an extensive knowledge of the Holy Scriptures tend to destroy the influence of false teachers?—2 Tim. iii. 16.

16. How shall these false teachers be known?
What is meant by *their fruits?* (Their conduct.)

INSTRUCTIONS OF THE SAVIOUR. 39

What question does Jesus ask?
What did he mean them to understand by that? (The conduct shows what principles actuate men.)
How is this related in Luke?—Luke vi. 44.

17, 18. How else did he express this?
How do men show whether they are evil or good?—Luke vi. 45.
What is one of the ways in which men show their character?—Matt. xii. 36, 37.
What did our Lord mean to represent by good trees and corrupt trees? (Good people and wicked people.)
If your actions are evil, what may you know of the state of your *heart?*

19. What is done to every tree that bringeth not forth good fruit?
Why is this done to it? (It is fit for nothing else.)
What did John the Baptist say when he began to preach?—Matt. iii. 10.
Is it only trees that bear bad fruit that are destroyed?—See Luke xiii. 6-9.
What does that parable teach? (That those who neglect their opportunities of being and doing good will be destroyed.)
What did our Lord say to his disciples?—John xv. 2.
What may be called good fruit?—Gal. v. 22, 23.

20. By what does our Lord again say false teachers shall be known?

21. What other caution did the Lord give?
Who are meant by those who say *Lord, Lord?* (Those who profess to be Christians.)
Does he say none of them shall enter in? (None shall enter whose profession is insincere.)
Who shall enter into his kingdom?
What must those who profess to love Jesus be careful to do?—Tit. iii. 8.
What is it to do the will of God?—Deut. xiii. 4.
Why are men unfit for heaven who do not obey God?—Matt. vi. 10; Ps. ciii. 20.
Why will it not do to profess to be Christians and yet not do the will of God?—1 John ii. 4.

22. What will many say to Christ in that day?
What day is meant by *that* day? (The Day of Judgment.)
As they have done these things, why will they not be accepted? (Because they have not done them for the glory of God.)

23. What will Jesus say to them?
What will our Lord mean by saying he "never knew them"? (Never approved them.)

Why will he bid them depart from him?
Repeat Psalm v. 4, 5.
Where must those go who are forced to depart from Jesus?—Matt. xxv. 41.

24. Whom does Christ liken to a wise man?
In what was this man wise?
What *sayings* are here meant? (Those things Jesus had just taught them.)

25. How was it seen that the house was firm?
Why did it not fall?
How is one who hears and does the commands of Christ like such a house? (His hopes rest on a sure foundation.)

26. Whom did Christ liken to a foolish man?
Why is such a man foolish? (In not securing a firm foundation.)
What did this foolish man do?
What do you suppose are represented by the rain, and floods, and winds, that beat upon that house? (Troubles and afflictions, death and judgment.)

27. What happened to the house?
Why did it fall?
What is there like this in the fate of sinners? (They will be destroyed, because their faith is not placed in the Rock of Ages.)
What will be their destruction?—Ps. ix. 17.
In what way alone are men safe?—1 Cor. iii. 11.

28. What is said of the people when Jesus had ended his sayings?
What is meant by his *doctrine?* (What he taught.)

29. Why were the people astonished?
How did Jesus teach as one having authority? (Having the authority of a law-giver.)
Who were the scribes? (Learned men whose duty it was to transcribe and teach the law.)
How did the scribes teach?—And see Matt. xv. 9.
You have now heard these sayings of Christ, what will be the consequence of your doing or not doing them?

LESSON XII.

The Parable of the Sower.

MATT. xiii. 1-9, 18.

1 The same day went Jesus out of the house, and sat by the sea side.
2 And great multitudes were gathered together unto him, so that he went into a ship, and sat; and the whole multitude stood on the shore.
3 And he spake many things unto them in parables, saying, Behold, a sower went forth to sow;
4 And when he sowed, some *seeds* fell by the way side, and the fowls came and devoured them up:
5 Some fell upon stony places, where they had not much earth: and forthwith they sprung up, because they had no deepness of earth:
6 And when the sun was up, they were scorched; and because they had no root, they withered away.
7 And some fell among thorns; and the thorns sprung up, and choked them:
8 But other fell into good ground, and brought forth fruit, some a hundredfold, some sixtyfold, some thirtyfold.
9 Who hath ears to hear, let him hear.
18 ¶ Hear ye therefore the parable of the sower.

1. WHERE did Jesus go?
What sea was this? (Sea of Galilee.)
2. Who came to him?
Where did he go then?
Where were the people?—Mark iv. 1.
3. How did Jesus speak to them?
What are *parables?* (Narratives given to illustrate some truth.)
Can you tell what was the advantage of teaching by parables? (It arrested the attention and enforced the truth.)
What is this parable about?
When did the Saviour explain this parable?—See ver. 10, 18, &c.
Where else is this parable recorded?—Mark iv. 3, &c.; Luke viii. 5, &c.
What is a *sower?* (One who sows seed.)
Who are represented by the sower?—See Mark
What is meant by the seed?—Luke viii. 11.
4. Where did some of the seeds fall?
What became of them?
Who are meant by those by the way side?—See ver. 19.
How is this told by Luke?—Luke viii. 12.
In what ways does Satan take away the Word? (By interesting the mind in something else.)
How are the young often prevented from attending to the commandments of God? (By irreligious companions and worldly amusements.)
Why is this no excuse for them?
What is every one's duty when thus tempted?—James iv. 7.

5. Where did other seed fall?
How soon did the seed spring up?
What is meant by *forthwith?* (Immediately.)
Why did they spring up so quickly?

6. What happened to them?
What then became of them?
How did Christ explain this?—Ver. 20, 21.
What is meant by *anon?* (Quickly.)
How is it told by Luke?—Luke viii. 13.
How does this kind of hearers differ from those from whom Satan took the word? (These take impulsive interest in it for a little while.)
What sort of persons who seem to be attentive to the word, have not the *root* in them? (Those whose hearts are not changed by it.)
What is meant by their being *offended?* (Turning away from religion.)
What caution does this give? (To see that our religion is rooted in faith in Christ.)

7. Among what did other seeds fall?
What became of them?
What is meant by the thorns *choking them?* (Preventing their growth.)
What is the meaning of this?—See ver. 22.
What is the *care of this world?* (Anxiety about worldly affairs.)
How does that prevent persons from attending to the word? (It occupies all their thoughts.)
What is the *deceitfulness of riches?* (Its delusive promises of good.)
How does that keep the truth from reaching the heart?—Deut. viii. 12–14.
What else does Mark mention?—Mark iv. 19.
What is meant by the *lusts of other things?* (Desires for worldly enjoyments.)
What does Luke call them?—Luke viii. 14.
What effect have they on the soul?—1 Pet. ii. 11.
How then should those who wish to serve God treat the *cares and riches and pleasures of this life?*—Phil. iv. 6; 1 Peter ii. 11.
What is Christ's rule?—Matt. vii. 20.
If then the hearers of the word produce *no* fruit, what are they known to be?—Luke xiv. 27.

8. What became of other seed?
What people are like that?—See ver. 23.
How are they further described?—Luke viii. 15.
What is meant by receiving the truth *in an honest and good heart?* (A heart which yields to its influence.)
What did they bring forth?

INSTRUCTIONS OF THE SAVIOUR. 43

What is meant by a *hundredfold, sixtyfold, &c.?* (A hundred grains or sixty grains for one.)

9. What did Jesus say to him who had ears to hear?
Is not this parable then addressed to *you* and to *all?*

Verse 18.

18. What are the words of Jesus written in this verse?
To whom was he speaking?—Ver. 10.
What did he mean here by *Hear ye?* (To call their attention.)
Why did he not explain the parable to the multitude?—Ver. 11-15.
What is meant by *keeping* it?—James i. 25.
How are they different in this respect from the first kind of hearers? (They bear fruit.)
What is the fruit they produce? (A holy life.)
How are Christians enabled to produce this fruit?—See John xv. 4, 5.
Can there be any piety without good fruit?—John xv. 8.
What is meant by some producing *a hundredfold, some sixtyfold, some thirtyfold?* (There are various degrees of fruitfulness among Christians.)
Who are now sowers of the word? (All who teach the Gospel.)
Has it not been taught to you?
If you have not received it in an honest and good heart, nor are showing it in your lives, will it do you any good?
What does the apostle say?—James i. 22.
What is this word able to do?—Acts xx. 32.
If any have been like the way side, or stony places, or thorny ground, in the parable, what should they now do?

LESSON XIII.

Parables of the hidden treasure; the pearl of great price; and the net.

MATT. xiii. 44-58.

44 ¶ Again, the kingdom of heaven is like unto treasure hid in a field; the which when a man hath found, he hideth, and for joy thereof goeth and selleth all that he hath, and buyeth that field.

45 ¶ Again, the kingdom of heaven is like unto a merchantman, seeking goodly pearls:
46 Who, when he had found one pearl of great price, went and sold all that he had, and bought it.

47 ¶ Again, the kingdom of heaven is like unto a net, that was cast into the sea, and gathered of every kind:
48 Which, when it was full, they drew to shore, and sat down, and gathered the good into vessels, but cast the bad away.
49 So shall it be at the end of the world: the angels shall come forth, and sever the wicked from among the just,
50 And shall cast them into the furnace of fire: there shall be wailing and gnashing of teeth.
51 Jesus saith unto them, Have ye understood all these things? They say unto him, Yea, Lord.
52 Then said he unto them, Therefore every scribe *which is* instructed unto the kingdom of heaven, is like unto a man *that is* a householder, which bringeth forth out of his treasure *things* new and old.

53 ¶ And it came to pass, *that* when Jesus had finished these parables, he departed thence.
54 And when he was come into his own country, he taught them in their synagogue, insomuch that they were astonished, and said, Whence hath this *man* this wisdom, and *these* mighty works?
55 Is not this the carpenter's son? Is not his mother called Mary? and his brethren, James, and Joses, and Simon, and Judas?
56 And his sisters, are they not all with us? Whence then hath this *man* all these things?
57 And they were offended in him. But Jesus said unto them, A prophet is not without honour, save in his own country, and in his own house.
58 And he did not many mighty works there because of their unbelief.

44. To what did Jesus compare the kingdom of heaven?
What is meant here by the kingdom of heaven? (The offer of salvation.)
What is *treasure?* (Something valuable; as silver or gold.)
What does our Lord say a man does when he finds this treasure?
Why does he buy the field? (To gain the treasure hidden in it.)
Why is the kingdom of heaven like treasure? (It is durable riches and happiness for eternity.)
What does David say in Ps. xix. 9, 10?
What is written in Prov. iii. 13–15?
Why should a man be willing to give every thing for such a treasure? (Because it is worth more. It is eternal life.)
Can it be bought?—Eph. ii. 8.
What is the invitation of the Bible?—Isa. lv. 1.
How is it to be obtained?—Isa. lv. 6, 7.

45, 46. To what does Jesus again liken the kingdom of heaven?
What is a *merchantman?* (One who buys and sells goods.)
What are *goodly pearls?* (Valuable pearls.)
What did he buy?
What did he give for it?
Why did he give so much for it? (He thought it so precious.)
What will those do who think religion to be worth more than every thing else?—Phil. iii. 8.
What does religion require us to give up?—Luke xiv. 33.

INSTRUCTIONS OF THE SAVIOUR.

47. What else did our Lord say the kingdom of heaven was like?
Every kind of *what?* (Of fish.)
How is Christ's kingdom, or his church here on earth, like this net? (All are not good who are gathered into it.)

48. What was done when the net was full?
What was done with the good?
What was done with the bad?

49. What shall be done like this at the end of the world?
What is the meaning of *sever?* (Separate.)
Who are the just? (True Christians.)
Why shall the wicked be separated from the just?—Rev. xxi. 27.

50. Where shall the wicked be cast?
What shall there be then?
What is meant by the furnace of fire?—Mark ix. 45.
What is wailing? (Lamentation.)
Why will they wail and gnash their teeth?—Rev. xiv. 10, 11.
Have not the wicked been often warned of this?—Luke xvi. 30, 31.

51. What did Jesus then ask the disciples?
What things did he mean? (The truths he had just taught them by parables.)
What reply did they make?

52. What did he next say to them?
What is here meant by every scribe who is instructed unto the kingdom of heaven? (Every one instructed in Gospel truths.)
What is a *householder?* (The head of a house.)
What is meant by his bringing forth out of his treasure things new and old? (Bringing out the various supplies as they were needed.)
How were the disciples to be like such a one? (In being ready to instruct others in the truths they had learned.)
What is the duty of all those who are well instructed in heavenly things? (To teach the ignorant.)
What command did Jesus give his disciples?—Matt. xxviii. 19, 20.

53. When Jesus had finished these parables, what did he do?
What parables? (Those seven which Jesus had just spoken.)

54. Into what country did he come?
Which part of the land was his own country?—Luke iv. 16.
Why is not Bethlehem called his own country? (Because he lived in Nazareth.)

Where did he teach at Nazareth?
What were the *synagogues* of the Jews? (Places of worship
What effect had his teaching on the people?
What did they say?

55. What else did they say concerning him?
Whom did they mean by the *carpenter?*—Luke iii. 23.

56. What farther did they say about Jesus?
How did these things prove that he had never received his wisdom from man? (He had not lived among the learned, but among poor and humble people.)

57. How did the people of Nazareth feel towards him?
What is meant by their being *offended in him?* (They rejected him.)
Why were they offended? (At his lowly life.)
What did Jesus say to them?
What did Jesus mean by this? (Others would believe in him, although his own city rejected him.)
Why is not a prophet or teacher likely to be well received in his own country? (He encounters more envy there than elsewhere.)

58. Why did Jesus not do many mighty works there?
What do you mean by *mighty works?* (Miracles.)
Why should this prevent his performing miracles? (They were too prejudiced to be convinced by them.)
Did he perform none at all?—See Mark vi. 5.
Is unbelief now as great a sin as when Christ was on earth? (Yes.)
What proof have we now of the truth of Christ's doctrines, which his hearers had not then?—John xiv. 29.
How are these things told by Mark?—Mark vi. 2–6.
Can we expect any blessing from God if we have not faith?—Heb. xi. 6.

LESSON XIV.

Jesus teaches humility, and shows his care for his people by the parable of the lost sheep.

MATT. xviii. 1–14.

1 At the same time came the disciples unto Jesus, saying, Who is the greatest in the kingdom of heaven?

2 And Jesus called a little child unto him, and set him in the midst of them,

3 And said, Verily I say unto you, Except ye be converted, and become as little children, ye shall not enter into the kingdom of heaven.

4 Whosoever therefore shall humble

INSTRUCTIONS OF THE SAVIOUR. 47

himself as this child, the same is greatest in the kingdom of heaven.

5 And whoso shall receive one such little child in my name receiveth me.

6 But whoso shall offend one of these little ones which believe in me, it were better for him that a millstone were hanged about his neck, and *that* he were drowned in the depth of the sea.

7 ¶ Woe unto the world because of offences! for it must needs be that offences come; but woe to that man by whom the offence cometh!

8 Wherefore if thy hand or thy foot offend thee, cut them off, and cast *them* from thee: it is better for thee to enter into life halt or maimed, rather than having two hands or two feet to be cast into everlasting fire.

9 And if thine eye offend thee, pluck it out, and cast *it* from thee: it is better for thee to enter into life with one eye, rather than having two eyes to be cast into hell fire.

10 Take heed that ye despise not one of these little ones; for I say unto you, That in heaven their angels do always behold the face of my Father which is in heaven.

11 For the Son of man is come to save that which was lost.

12 How think ye? If a man have a hundred sheep, and one of them be gone astray, doth he not leave the ninety and nine, and goeth into the mountains, and seeketh that which is gone astray?

13 And if so be that he find it, verily I say unto you, he rejoiceth more of that *sheep*, than of the ninety and nine which went not astray.

14 Even so it is not the will of your Father which is in heaven, that one of these little ones should perish.

1. WHAT did the disciples ask Jesus?
What took place before they asked the question?—See Mark ix. 33-35.
What did they mean by it? (Who should be first in the kingdom Jesus was about to establish.)
What sort of a kingdom is it probable they thought Christ's would be? (A temporal one.)
What sort of a kingdom is it? (Spiritual.)

2. What did Jesus do?
What then did he do with the child?—Mark ix. 36.

3. What did Jesus say?
What is it to be *converted?* (To be changed or turned.)
In what respect must those who are converted become like little children? (They must be humble and obedient.)
Does it mean that children are so good that it is only necessary to be like them? (No.)
What had the disciples asked?—Verse 1.
What character did that show in them? (Proud and ambitious.)
How then was it reproved by what Christ said? (He told them they must have the humility of a little child.)
Why must we be humble, and obedient, and dependent, if we would enter the kingdom of heaven? (Because that is the spirit of heaven.)
At what other time did Jesus speak this?—Matt. xix. 13-15.

4. Who did Jesus say was greatest in the kingdom of heaven?
What is it to be humble? (Not to estimate ourselves highly.)
On whom does a little child depend for the supply of its wants? (Its parents.)

On whom does the humble man depend for every favour?—
(On his Father in heaven.)
What is written about the humble in Isaiah lvii. 15?

5. What does Jesus declare in this verse?
What sort of a person is meant by "one such little child"? (One with such a spirit.)
How is this told by the other writers?—Mark ix. 37; Luke ix. 48.
What is it to receive such in Christ's name? (To love them and treat them kindly, because they are followers of Christ.)
What does Jesus mean by saying that whosoever does so, receives *him?* (Jesus will accept it as if it were done to him.)
What will he say at the last day to those who have been kind to his people for his sake?—Matt. xxv. 34-40.
What did he say to John?—Mark ix. 41.

6. What did Christ say of those who should offend such?
What is meant by *offending* them?—See Rom. xiv. 13, last clause.
What is written in Psalm cxxv. of the Lord's care over his people?
What is the sin of tempting any of God's children to do wrong?
—1 Cor. iii. 16.

7. Why did our Lord pronounce woe unto the world?
What is meant by *offences* here?—See Rom. xiv. 13, last clause.
How is this explained by the next verse? (It shows that offences mean temptations to sin.)
What is added in this verse?
What is meant by *it must needs be?* (It is unavoidable.)
What is meant by *woe to that man?* (He will incur punishment.)
What is the sin of causing others to fall? (It is serving Satan.)
—1 Peter v. 8.
How is this often done? (By evil example.—Heb. xii. 13.)
What does this teach us about the danger of bad company?—
1 Cor. xv. 33.

8, 9. How did the Lord enforce this?
Had he ever said this before?—See Matt. v. 29, 30.
What is meant by cutting off a hand or foot, &c., that offends? (Giving up every thing that tempts to sin.)
What is the meaning of *halt* or *maimed?* (Halt means lame; maimed, having lost limbs.)
What is the simple meaning of these two verses? (That we had better sacrifice every earthly good than lose heaven.)
Should you not be willing to give up any thing rather than commit sin, or cause others to sin?
How does Christ here speak of the future punishment of the wicked?
How is this spoken of in the account given by Mark?—Mark ix. 43, 44.

INSTRUCTIONS OF THE SAVIOUR. 49

How long then will their punishment continue?—2 Thess. i. 9.
What do you read in Rom. viii. 13?

10. What caution has Christ given respecting our treatment of his little ones?
What is meant by despising them? (Treating with contempt.)
What does he say of their angels?
What is one of the employments of angels?—Heb. i. 14.

11. For what purpose did the Son of man come?
Who is the *Son of man?* (The Lord Jesus Christ.)
Who are meant by the lost? (Sinners.)
Why are men said to be lost?—Eph. ii. 1; Gen. vi. 12.
How does the Son of man save the lost?—Isa. liii. 5; Mark x. 45.
What has he done that he might save sinners?—1 Cor. xv. 3.

12. What parable did the Lord speak?
Whom does our Lord mean to represent by the sheep gone astray? (Sinners.)
What is to be understood by the owner's going into the mountains to seek it? (Christ coming to save sinners.)
How does David speak of himself in Ps. cxix. 176?
Can you mention any places in which Christ is spoken of as a shepherd?—Zech. xiii. 7; 1 Peter ii. 25; John x.

13. What does Jesus say of the man if he find the sheep?
Why do you suppose he would rejoice more over that sheep than over the others? (It had been rescued from danger.)
What does this teach you of the feelings of God towards repenting, returning sinners?
What other parable did our Lord speak on this subject?—See Luke xv. 8-10.

14. How does Jesus here teach us the meaning of this parable?
What is it to *perish?* (To be destroyed.)
What else does this parable teach?—Luke xv. 7.
What message did the Lord send to his people as in Ezek. xxxiii. 11?

LESSON XV.

Peter's question, how often he should forgive his brother—Christ's instruction about brotherly love.

MATT. xviii. 21-35.

21 ¶ Then came Peter to him, and said, Lord, how oft shall my brother sin against me, and I forgive him? till seven times?
22 Jesus saith unto him, I say not unto thee, Until seven times: but, Until seventy times seven.
23 ¶ Therefore is the kingdom of heaven likened unto a certain king, which would take account of his servants.
24 And when he had begun to reckon, one was brought unto him, which owed him ten thousand talents.
25 But forasmuch as he had not to pay, his lord commanded him to be sold, and his wife, and children, and all that he had, and payment to be made.
26 The servant therefore fell down, and worshipped him, saying, Lord, have patience with me, and I will pay thee all.
27 Then the lord of that servant was moved with compassion, and loosed him, and forgave him the debt.
28 But the same servant went out, and found one of his fellow servants, which owed him a hundred pence; and he laid hands on him, and took *him* by the throat, saying, Pay me that thou owest.
29 And his fellow servant fell down at his feet, and besought him, saying, Have patience with me, and I will pay thee all.
30 And he would not: but went and cast him into prison, till he should pay the debt.
31 So when his fellow servants saw what was done, they were very sorry, and came and told unto their lord all that was done.
32 Then his lord, after that he had called him, said unto him, O thou wicked servant, I forgave thee all that debt, because thou desiredst me:
33 Shouldest not thou also have had compassion on thy fellow servant, even as I had pity on thee?
34 And his lord was wroth, and delivered him to the tormenters, till he should pay all that was due unto him.
35 So likewise shall my heavenly Father do also unto you, if ye from your hearts forgive not every one his brother their trespasses.

21. WHAT did Peter ask Christ?
What is the meaning of *forgive?* (To overlook an offence,—to pardon it.)
Whom did Peter mean by his brother? (His fellow-men.)

22. How did Jesus answer Peter?
What is it probable our Lord meant by "seventy times seven"?
—And see Gen. iv. 24. (Times without number.)
What is written in Col. iii. 13?
What had our Lord said before on the subject of forgiveness?
—Matt. vi. 14, 15.
In what manner are we required to ask forgiveness of God?—Matt. vi. 12.

23. What did Jesus say the kingdom of heaven was like?
What is meant here by the kingdom of heaven? (The church of God.)

INSTRUCTIONS OF THE SAVIOUR. 51

What is meant by the king's *taking account* of his servants? (Settling their affairs.)
Are not all the officers of a king usually called his servants? (Yes.)

24. How much did one owe him?
What was the value of a talent? (The Hebrew talent of silver was about $1,740; of gold, $17,400; the Greek talent of silver was about $960; of gold, $9,600.

25. Could the servant pay his debt?
What did the king command?
Was this permitted by the Jewish law?—Lev. xxv. 39, 40.

26. What did the servant do?
What is the meaning of *worshipped* here?—See Luke xiv. 10.

27. How did his master then feel?
What did he do for him?

28. What did that servant immediately do?
How much is "an hundred pence"? (About fifteen dollars.)
Did he ask for it in a proper manner? (No.)

29. What did his fellow servant do?
What is the meaning of *besought?* (Entreated.)
What did he promise?

30. What did the other servant do?

31. What did his fellow servants do?
What lord was this?—See ver. 23.

32. What did the king say to him?
How much had he forgiven him?—Verse 24.

33. What should he have done?
How much did his fellow servant owe him?—Verse 28.
Why was this a reason for his having pity on him? (He should have been merciful to others to manifest his gratitude.)

34. What did his master do?
How long was he to be punished?
Why was he treated in this manner? (His conduct proved him unworthy of forgiveness.)

35. What does this parable teach?
In what respect is a sinner like the servant who owed more than he could pay? (In being unable to atone for his sins.)
What do men owe to God?—Job vii. 20.
If he should call them to account, could they give any excuse for not being able to pay?—Rom. iii. 19.
What are we taught of the sins of men against each other, in comparison with those of men against God?—See ver. 24 and 28.

Why then should we forgive men their sins?—Eph. iv. 32.
How must we forgive?
What is it to forgive *from the heart?* (Sincerely.)
If God has forgiven Christians so much, how should they love him?—See Luke vii. 47.
When will God bring all men to their *account* for these things? —Rev. xx. 12.
Is any one prepared for the judgment who does not love all men?—1 John iii. 14.

LESSON XVI.

Jesus shows a certain lawyer, by the story of the good Samaritan, who is his neighbour.

LUKE x. 25-37.

25 ¶ And, behold, a certain lawyer stood up, and tempted him, saying, Master, what shall I do to inherit eternal life?
26 He said unto him, What is written in the law? how readest thou?
27 And he answering said, Thou shalt love the Lord thy God with all thy heart, and with all thy soul, and with all thy strength, and with all thy mind; and thy neighbour as thyself.
28 And he said unto him, Thou hast answered right: this do, and thou shalt live.
29 But he, willing to justify himself, said unto Jesus, And who is my neighbour?
30 And Jesus answering said, A certain *man* went down from Jerusalem to Jericho, and fell among thieves, which stripped him of his raiment, and wounded *him*, and departed, leaving *him* half dead.
31 And by chance there came down a certain priest that way; and when he saw him, he passed by on the other side.
32 And likewise a Levite, when he was at the place, came and looked *on him*, and passed by on the other side.
33 But a certain Samaritan, as he journeyed, came where he was; and when he saw him, he had compassion *on him*,
34 And went to *him*, and bound up his wounds, pouring in oil and wine, and set him on his own beast, and brought him to an inn, and took care of him.
35 And on the morrow when he departed, he took out two pence, and gave *them* to the host, and said unto him, Take care of him: and whatsoever thou spendest more, when I come again, I will repay thee.
36 Which now of these three, thinkest thou, was neighbour unto him that fell among the thieves?
37 And he said, He that shewed mercy on him. Then said Jesus unto him, Go, and do thou likewise.

25. WHO tempted Christ?
What was the employment of lawyers among the Jews? (To transcribe, study, and explain the law of the Old Testament.)
What is meant here by *tempted?* (Tried to lead him into some contradiction of the law.)
Did the lawyer really wish to learn from Christ? (No.)
Why did he call Jesus *master?* (It was a title given to their teachers.)

INSTRUCTIONS OF THE SAVIOUR. 53

Why did the Pharisees, scribes, and lawyers, so frequently ask questions of our Saviour?—Luke xi. 53, 54.
Did they ever detect him in doing or saying any thing that was sinful or improper?—1 Peter ii. 22.

26. What did Jesus say to him?
What did he mean by *the law?* (The Scriptures.)
Why did Jesus refer this man to the law? (To make him see that he had not met its requirements.)

27. What answer did the lawyer make?
In what parts of the Old Testament are these words?—Deut. vi. 5, and Lev. xix. 18.
Was this all the law? (No.)

28. What did Jesus say to the lawyer?
What had Jesus himself said of these two commandments?—Matt. xxii. 40.
What did Jesus mean by *thou shalt live?* (Have eternal life.)
Has *any* one kept this law perfectly?—Ps. xiv. 2, 3.
What do you learn from Rom. iii. 19, 20?
Why is it that no one keeps the perfect law of God?—Rom. viii. 7.
What is said about the law in Rom. vii. 12?
Have we any excuse for not keeping God's law? (No.)
What is said, in Gal. iii. 10, about him who breaks it?
How can sinners who are continually breaking it obtain eternal life?—Gal. iii. 13.
Does that free them from the obligation to obey the law?—2 Peter iii. 1, 2.
What did Christ himself say?—Matt. v. 17.

29. What did the lawyer wish to do?
What is meant by *justifying himself?* (Showing that he had kept the law.)
What did he ask Jesus?
What had the Lord been saying about neighbours?—Verses 27, 28.

30. How did Jesus answer the lawyer?
What did our Lord mean by relating the parable to the lawyer? (To answer his question.)
Where was the man going?
What was this road remarkable for?*

31. While the man was lying there, who came that way?
What was a priest? (One who officiated in the temple service.)
What did he do?

---

* See Geography of the Bible, published by the American Sunday-School Union, page 92.

5*

Why did he go on the opposite side?

32. Who came next to the place?
What was the difference between a priest and a Levite? (The priests only offered sacrifice and burnt incense, the Levites assisted them.)—1 Chron. xxiii. 27–30.
What did the Levite do?
What was the sin of these two men? (Selfishness.)

33. Who next came along?
Who were the Samaritans? (A people of Assyrian descent, living in Samaria.)
What opinion had the Jews of the Samaritans? (They hated and despised them.)
What is said of the Samaritan when he saw the man?
What does this teach you when you see any one in distress?

34. How did the good Samaritan *show* his compassion?
What does this conduct of the Samaritan teach you?—Heb. xiii. 16.

35. What did he do on the morrow when he departed?
How much was two pence? (About thirty cents.)
What did he say to the host?
Who is meant by the *host?* (The innkeeper.)

36. What question did Jesus ask the lawyer?
What three did he mean?
What question had the lawyer asked, to which this parable was an answer? (Who is my neighbour?)

37. What did the lawyer say?
Who was that? (The Samaritan.)
How did this parable answer the lawyer's question? (It shows that we must regard as our neighbour any one from whom we receive good, or to whom we can do good.)
How does it teach that we should be kind even to those who despise us, or are our enemies? (By the example of the Samaritan.)
How would many have acted if they had had such an opportunity as the Samaritan had of letting an enemy suffer?
How did Jesus exhort the lawyer?
In what ways can we do likewise? (In doing all the kindness we can to every one.)
What should be our resolution from every good example in God's word? (To do likewise.)
Can you tell from this who is your neighbour?

LESSON XVII.

Our Lord rebukes the wickedness of the Scribes and Pharisees.

LUKE xi. 37-44.

37 ¶ And as he spake, a certain Pharisee besought him to dine with him: and he went in, and sat down to meat.
38 And when the Pharisee saw it, he marvelled that he had not first washed before dinner.
39 And the Lord said unto him, Now do ye Pharisees make clean the outside of the cup and the platter; but your inward part is full of ravening and wickedness.
40 Ye fools, did not he that made that which is without make that which is within also?
41 But rather give alms of such things as ye have; and, behold, all things are clean unto you.
42 But woe unto you, Pharisees! for ye tithe mint and rue and all manner of herbs, and pass over judgment and the love of God: these ought ye to have done, and not to leave the other undone.
43 Woe unto you, Pharisees! for ye love the uppermost seats in the synagogues, and greetings in the markets.
44 Woe unto you, scribes and Pharisees, hypocrites! for ye are as graves which appear not, and the men that walk over *them* are not aware *of them*.

37. WITH whom did Jesus dine?
38. What did the Pharisee wonder at?
Why did the Pharisee suppose that Jesus would wash before dinner?—Mark vii. 3.
Was this required of them by the law of God? (No.)
39. What did the Lord say to him?
What did he mean by this? (If the cup were filled by extortion the ceremonious washing would be useless.)
What is *ravening?* (Rapacious desire.)
How did the Pharisees act that was like this? (They were strict in outward ceremonies while their lives were wicked.)
What did Christ say of them?—Matt. xxiii. 23-27.
What is the meaning of these comparisons?—See Matt. xxiii. 28.
40. What did Jesus call the Pharisees?
What was foolish in their conduct? (They did not care to be religious in heart, but only to appear so to men.)
What question did Jesus ask?
Explain that question? (It implies that as God made both body and soul, he can see the condition of both.)
Can God be deceived by outward appearances, or pleased by actions that are only good in appearance?—1 Sam. xvi. 7.
What does God require besides attention to outward duties?—Mark xii. 33.
How did this remark of the Saviour apply to what the Pharisee had wondered at?—See ver. 38.
41. What did Jesus bid the Pharisees do?
What is it to *give alms?* (To give to the poor.)

What did he add?
Did he mean that this would make all their conduct holy? (No.)
Can men give alms without loving their fellow men?—See 1 Cor. xiii. 3.
What then did the Lord mean? (If they were penitent for their former lives they would show it by doing good with their property.)

42. What did Jesus tell the Pharisees?
What is meant by *woe unto you?* (Punishment awaits you.)
What is the meaning of *tithe?* (A tenth part.)
Did the law require the Jews to pay tithes?—See Lev. xxvii. 30.
How did the Jews show their strictness in keeping this part of the law?
What did they omit?
How is this expressed in Matthew?—Matt. xxiii. 23, 24.
What does this teach us? (That our first duty is to God.)
What does the Lord prefer to all outward services?—See Isa. i. 16, 17.
What did our Lord say they ought to have done? (Judgment and the love of God.)
What should they not have left undone? (The smallest duties.)

43. What did Jesus again say to the Pharisees?
What did they love?
What were the *uppermost seats* in the *synagogues?* (The most conspicuous.)
What is meant by "greetings in the markets"? (Receiving marks of respect in public.)
What sort of a spirit did this show? (Proud and selfish.)
Repeat Phil. ii. 3.
What will be done to him who exalts himself?—Luke xiv. 11.

44. To whom did Jesus then speak besides the Pharisees?
Who were the scribes? (Authorized teachers of the law.)
What did he call them?
What is a *hypocrite?* (One who assumes a false appearance.)
What was part of their hypocrisy?—See Matt. xxiii. 3, 5.
To what did Jesus liken these men?
In what respect were the scribes and Pharisees like hidden graves? (They were careful in their outward conduct, while their hearts were full of iniquity.)
Of what were those in danger who kept company with them? (Of becoming like them.)
In what respect are hypocrites more dangerous than other men? (They exert an evil influence before it is suspected.)

INSTRUCTIONS OF THE SAVIOUR. 57

LESSON XVIII.

Subject continued.

WHAT was the subject of the last lesson?
What did the Lord say of the Pharisees?

LUKE xi. 45-54.

45 ¶ Then answered one of the lawyers, and said unto him, Master, thus saying thou reproachest us also.
46 And he said, Woe unto you also, ye lawyers! for ye lade men with burdens grievous to be borne, and ye yourselves touch not the burdens with one of your fingers.
47 Woe unto you! for ye build the sepulchres of the prophets, and your fathers killed them.
48 Truly ye bear witness that ye allow the deeds of your fathers: for they indeed killed them, and ye build their sepulchres.
49 Therefore also said the wisdom of God, I will send them prophets and apostles, and *some* of them they shall slay and persecute:
50 That the blood of all the prophets, which was shed from the foundation of the world, may be required of this generation;
51 From the blood of Abel unto the blood of Zacharias, which perished between the altar and the temple: verily I say unto you, It shall be required of this generation.
52 Woe unto you, lawyers! for ye have taken away the key of knowledge: ye entered not in yourselves, and them that were entering in ye hindered.
53 And as he said these things unto them, the scribes and the Pharisees began to urge *him* vehemently, and to provoke him to speak of many things;
54 Laying wait for him, and seeking to catch something out of his mouth, that they might accuse him.

45. Who then spoke to Jesus?
What did he say?
What is the meaning of *reproachest?* (Dost censure.)
How did it reproach them as well as the others? (Because they did those very things.)
Does it seem that they were Pharisees also?—Compare Matt. xxiii. 2, 4.

46. What did Jesus then say to them?
What did he tell them of their doings?
What was meant by the *burdens* which the lawyers laid upon the people? (Religious ceremonies.)
What should those who require much of others be careful to do themselves?—Rom. ii. 21-23; Titus ii. 7, 8.

47. What did the lawyers do?
Who killed the prophets?
What are *sepulchres?* (Tombs.)
Who were the *prophets?* (Those who were sent by God to communicate his word to the people.)
Why did the Jews persecute and kill the prophets? (For rebuking their sins.)
What is written concerning this, in 2 Chron. xxxvi. 15, 16?
Why did they build sepulchres for the prophets whom their fathers had killed? (Professedly to render honour to their memory.)

How did Christ speak of their hypocrisy in this?—Matt. xxiii. 29-32.

48. Of what did Jesus tell them they bore witness?
How did they bear witness to, or prove this?
What is meant by allowing the deeds of their fathers? (Approving them.)
How did their actions prove that they were of the same spirit with their fathers? (They persecuted Jesus and his apostles.)

49. What did "therefore the wisdom of God" say?
What is meant here by *the wisdom of God?* (Jesus Christ.—1 Cor. i. 30.)
When did the Lord Jesus send them prophets and apostles?—Luke x. 1-3; Matt. x. 2-5.
How would they be treated?—Matt. xxiii. 34.
In what book of the New Testament do you read how the words of our Lord were proved true? (The Acts.)
Of which of his apostles do you particularly find an account? —Acts vii. 59, and xii. 1, 2.
What did Stephen tell the Jews?—Acts vii. 51, 52.
How does the apostle Paul speak of his persecutions?—2 Cor. xi. 24, 25.

50. What did Jesus farther say of that generation?
What is meant by the blood of the prophets being required of that generation? (The judgments they deserved for shedding their blood were coming upon them.)

51. Who is mentioned here as the first prophet that was killed for the truth's sake?
Who killed Abel?—Gen. iv. 8.
Why did Cain kill him?—See 1 John iii. 12.
Is it known what Zacharias is meant here? (Not certainly.)
What Zacharias is mentioned in the Old Testament as having been slain?—2 Chron. xxiv. 20, 21.
How may all this blood be said to have come upon that generation to which Christ spoke? (In the punishment they suffered.)
What did the Jews themselves say when they were going to crucify Christ?—Matt. xxvii. 25.
What is meant by *this generation?* (Those then living.)
What signal punishment came upon the Jews soon after this? (The destruction of Jerusalem.)
What may *we* learn from the vengeance of God which came at last upon the Jews?—Prov. xxix. 1.
What do you learn concerning this in Rom. xi. 20-23?

52. What did our Lord again say to the lawyers?
What is meant by their having taken away the *key of knowledge?* (They had given false interpretations of the Scriptures.)

What was the peculiar business of the scribes and lawyers? (To explain the law.)
How did they hinder the people from entering in? (By false teaching respecting the prophecies relating to the Messiah.)
How should we treat a false teacher?—2 John 10, 11.

53. As Jesus said these things, what did the scribes and Pharisees do?
What is the meaning of *vehemently?* (Earnestly.)
What did they wish him to do?

54. What was their object in this?
What is meant by *laying wait* for him? (Trying to ensnare him into saying something wrong.)
Why did they want to accuse Jesus?—Luke xxii 2.
What do you learn from this lesson to have been the general character of the scribes and Pharisees? (Wicked and hypocritical.)
What particular sins does it warn you against? (Pride and hypocrisy.)
Why were the scribes and Pharisees so much opposed to the gospel?—John vii. 7.

LESSON XIX.

The Parable of the Tares.

MATT. xiii. 24-30. (36-43).

24 ¶ Another parable put he forth unto them, saying, The kingdom of heaven is likened unto a man which sowed good seed in his field;
25 But while men slept, his enemy came and sowed tares among the wheat, and went his way.
26 But when the blade was sprung up, and brought forth fruit, then appeared the tares also.
27 So the servants of the householder came and said unto him, Sir, didst not thou sow good seed in thy field? from whence then hath it tares?
28 He said unto them, An enemy hath done this. The servants said unto him, Wilt thou then that we go and gather them up?
29 But he said, Nay; lest, while ye gather up the tares, ye root up also the wheat with them.
30. Let both grow together until the harvest: and in the time of harvest I will say to the reapers, Gather ye together first the tares, and bind them in bundles to burn them: but gather the wheat into my barn.
36 ¶ Then Jesus sent the multitude away, and went into the house; and his disciples came unto him, saying, Declare unto us the parable of the tares of the field.
37 He answered and said unto them, He that soweth the good seed is the Son of man;
38 The field is the world; the good seed are the children of the kingdom; but the tares are the children of the wicked *one;*
39 The enemy that sowed them is the devil; the harvest is the end of the world, and the reapers are the angels.
40 As therefore the tares are gathered and burned in the fire; so shall it be in the end of this world.

41 The Son of man shall send forth his angels, and they shall gather out of his kingdom all things that offend, and them which do iniquity,

42 And shall cast them into a furnace of fire: there shall be wailing and gnashing of teeth.

43 Then shall the righteous shine forth as the sun in the kingdom of their Father. Who hath ears to hear, let him hear.

24. WHAT parable is written here?
When did Jesus explain this parable?—See ver. 36.
Who is represented by the man sowing good seed?—Ver. 37.
What is the *field?*—Ver. 38.
What is the *good seed?*—Ver. 38.
Why is the field called *the world?*—And see Mark xvi. 15.
How may *the Lord* be said to sow this field? (By causing his word to be published.)

25. What took place while men slept?
What are *tares?* (A kind of worthless, poisonous wheat.)
Who are represented by the tares?—Ver. 38.
Who is the *enemy* that sows them?—Ver. 39.
How does Satan sow them? (By introducing false doctrines and deceiving men about themselves.)
What is meant by his sowing them *while men slept?* (Secretly and unobserved.)
Why are the wicked among the righteous like tares among wheat? (Their influence is injurious, yet their outward acts are often similar to those of Christians.)
Why are sinners called the children of the wicked one?—See 1 John iii. 8.

26. When did the tares appear?
What is meant by the *blade?* (The leaf.)

27. What did the servants of the sower say to him?

28. What did he say to his servants?
What did the servants offer to do?
Why did they wish to gather them up? (Because they injured the wheat.)

29. How did he answer them?

30. What did he say should be done?
What is represented by the harvest?—Ver. 39.
How is the end of the world like the harvest? (The good and the bad will all be gathered; the one to be saved, and the other destroyed.)
What should then be done?
Who are called the reapers?—Ver. 39.
Will the angels be present in the judgment?—Matt. xxv. 31.
What should be done with the tares?
Why are tares burned? (They are worthless.)
What will be like this in the end of the world?—Ver. 40.

INSTRUCTIONS OF THE SAVIOUR. 61

What will then take place?—Ver. 41, 43.
What was to be done with the wheat in the harvest?
What shall be like this in the judgment?—Ver. 43.
In what other manner did Christ speak of this time?—See Matt. xxv. 34, 41.
How had Daniel spoken of it?—Dan. xii. 2, 3.
What do you learn from this parable of the reason why God permits the evil and the good alike to live in the world?—(To show his forbearance, and to teach it to his people.)
What encouragement should Christians take from this to persuade sinners to repentance?—2 Peter iii. 9.
What is said to Christians in the epistle of Jude?—Jude 20-23.
What encouragement does the forbearance of God give to sinners to turn to Christ now? (It proves to them that God is willing to save.)
What did the apostle Paul say to the Athenians?—Acts xvii. 30, 31.
What may this parable teach us about persons appearing to be Christians, and being with them in the church of Christ, and yet who may be deceiving themselves and others? (Their true character will be manifested at the judgment.)
Who is the Judge that will direct the angels to separate the good from the bad? (Our Lord Jesus Christ.)
What did John the Baptist declare of Christ?—Matt. iii. 12.
What did Jesus say as he closed this parable?
What is meant by that? (Let all who hear, heed.)
As you have heard this solemn warning, what is *your* duty?

LESSON XX.

Jesus warns his disciples against hypocrisy and the fear of man—The parable of the Covetous Rich Man.

LUKE xii. 1-10. 15-21.

1 In the mean time, when there were gathered together an innumerable multitude of people, insomuch that they trode one upon another, he began to say unto his disciples first of all, Beware ye of the leaven of the Pharisees, which is hypocrisy.

2 For there is nothing covered, that shall not be revealed; neither hid, that shall not be known.

3 Therefore, whatsoever ye have spoken in darkness shall be heard in the light; and that which ye have spoken in the ear in closets shall be proclaimed upon the housetops.

4 And I say unto you my friends, Be not afraid of them that kill the body, and after that have no more that they can do.

5 But I will forewarn you whom ye shall fear: Fear him, which after he hath killed hath power to cast into hell; yea, I say unto you, Fear him.

6 Are not five sparrows sold for two

PARABLES AND OTHER

farthings, and not one of them is forgotten before God?

7 But even the very hairs of your head are all numbered. Fear not therefore: ye are of more value than many sparrows.

8 Also I say unto you, Whosoever shall confess me before men, him shall the Son of man also confess before the angels of God:

9 But he that denieth me before men shall be denied before the angels of God.

10 And whosoever shall speak a word against the Son of man, it shall be forgiven him: but unto him that blasphemeth against the Holy Ghost it shall not be forgiven.

15 And he said unto them, Take heed, and beware of covetousness: for a man's life consisteth not in the abundance of the things which he possesseth.

16 And he spake a parable unto them, saying, The ground of a certain rich man brought forth plentifully:

17 And he thought within himself, saying, What shall I do, because I have no room where to bestow my fruits?

18 And he said, This will I do: I will pull down my barns, and build greater; and there will I bestow all my fruits and my goods.

19 And I will say to my soul, Soul, thou hast much goods laid up for many years; take thine ease, eat, drink, *and* be merry.

20 But God said unto him, *Thou* fool, this night thy soul shall be required of thee; then whose shall those things be, which thou hast provided?

21 So *is* he that layeth up treasure for himself, and is not rich toward God.

1. How great a multitude were gathered together to hear Jesus?
To whom did Jesus begin to speak?
What did he say?
What is it to *beware?* (To take care to avoid.)
What is *hypocrisy?* (Appearing to be what we are not.)
What is *leaven?* (That which produces fermentation.)
Why did he call hypocrisy the *leaven* of the Pharisees? (It pervaded and influenced their actions.)
What did Christ once say to his disciples?—Matt. xvi. 6.

2. What did Jesus go on to say?
What does hypocrisy try to cover? (Wickedness.)
What is the meaning of *revealed?* (Made known.)
When will every thing be revealed?—Rev. xx. 12; Rom. ii. 16.
What then shows the folly as well as the sin of hypocrisy?—Jer. xvii. 10.

3. What else shall be made known?
How was this applied to the twelve apostles?—Matt. x. 27.
What is its meaning? (The truths Jesus had taught them in private they were to teach publicly.)
If it refers to the preaching of the gospel, how is it true? (At first, through the persecution of its enemies, the Gospel was preached privately, now it is openly proclaimed.)
If it refers to their most secret words being made known, how is it true?—Eccl. xii. 14.

4. What did Jesus call his disciples here?
Whom did Jesus say are his friends?—John xv. 14.
Of whom did he tell them not to be afraid?
How would the disciples be in danger of such treatment? (They would be persecuted for Jesus's sake.)

INSTRUCTIONS OF THE SAVIOUR. 63

What did Jesus tell his disciples about this?—Matt. x. 17, 18.
What is meant by the saying, "after that have no more that they can do"?—See Matt. x. 28.

5. Whom does our Lord forewarn them to fear?
What is the meaning of *forewarn?* (Admonish beforehand.)
Whom did Jesus mean? (God.)
Why should they fear him?—And see Matt. x. 28.
How did Peter and John show that they did not fear what their enemies could do to them?—Acts iv. 18-20.

6. What did Jesus say of God's care for his creatures?
How is this expressed in Matthew?—Matt. x. 29.
What was the value of *two farthings?* (Between two and three cents.)
Though they are of so little value, what does he say of the care of God for them?

7. What other instance did he give?
What did he teach them by this? (That God by his providence cared for their smallest interests.)
Why does he bid them not fear?
Why should they not fear?—Heb. xiii. 6.
Why are men of more value than many sparrows? (They have immortal souls.)

8. What did the Lord then say?
What is it to confess Christ before men? (To profess faith in Christ as our Saviour.)
When ought you to confess him before men? (Always, in all our lives.)
How shall the Son of man confess such before the angels of God?—Matt. xxv. 34.

9. What does he say to him that denieth him before men?
What is it to deny Christ before men? (To show no obedience or love to him.)
Why do people deny Christ?
Of what were the disciples in danger if they confessed Christ before the heathen? (Of persecution and death.)
How shall Christ deny those who deny him?—Matt. vii. 23.

10. What is said of him who shall speak a word against the Son of man?
Does this mean that every such person shall be forgiven? (No.)
What does it mean? (That those who repent of this sin will be forgiven.)
What sin did our Lord say shall not be forgiven?
What is it to **blaspheme?** (To speak impiously or profanely of God.)

Can you tell on what occasion Christ said this?—Mark iii. 22, 29.
How had the Pharisees on that occasion spoken against the Holy Ghost? (They had attributed to the power of Satan the miracles performed by the power of the Holy Ghost.)
Why did the Lord say this?—Mark iii. 30.
What may this teach us? (To be very careful never to speak irreverent words.)

Verses 15-21.

15. What did the Lord say to the people?
What led him to say this?—See ver. 13.
What is *covetousness?* (Excessive desire of wealth, or of what belongs to another.)
Why should we beware of covetousness?
What is meant by this saying? (Life does not depend upon it.)
Can riches make a man happy if he has other things to distress him?—Eccles. vi. 1, 2.
Can riches prolong a man's life?—Ps. xlix. 6-10.
What is the sin of covetousness? (It is a transgression of God's commandment.)
What is the tenth commandment?—Ex. xx. 17.
What is the danger of desiring to be rich?—1 Tim. vi. 9, 10.

16. What did the Lord then tell them?
How does it begin?

17. What did the rich man say?
What ought he to have done with his fruits?—Prov. iii. 9; 1 John iii. 17.
What is the apostle's advice?—2 Cor. ix. 8, 9.

18. But what did he say he would do?
What did the Lord Jesus say about laying up treasures on earth?—Matt. vi. 19.
Repeat 1 Tim. vi. 17, 18.

19. What did he intend to do?
What was foolish in this? (He had placed his hopes of happiness on earthly things, and made no preparation for eternity.)
What was sinful? (He was ungrateful to God and selfish.)
What use should we make of all our time? (To love God and do and be good.)
Why has not a man a *right* to spend his riches and his time in eating, drinking, and being merry?—Ps. c. 3; Rom. xiv. 8.
How does Solomon warn the young on this subject?—Eccl. xi. 9.

20. What did God say to this man?
What is meant by his soul being required of him? (He should die.)
What question is asked here?

INSTRUCTIONS OF THE SAVIOUR.

Why were his riches no longer his own?—1 Tim. 6, 7.

21. What did our Lord add in this verse?
What is it to lay up treasure for one's self? (To gain wealth for our own use.)
What is it to be rich towards God? (To labour for his glory and the good of our fellow men.)
Why cannot a man do both these things?—Luke xvi. 13.
What is your first duty?—See ver. 31.

LESSON XXI.

The duty of being ready for the coming of the Lord.

LUKE xii. 35-48.

35 Let your loins be girded about, and *your* lights burning;
36 And ye yourselves like unto men that wait for their lord, when he will return from the wedding; that, when he cometh and knocketh, they may open unto him immediately.
37 Blessed *are* those servants, whom the lord when he cometh shall find watching: verily I say unto you, that he shall gird himself, and make them to sit down to meat, and will come forth and serve them.
38 And if he shall come in the second watch, or come in the third watch, and find *them* so, blessed are those servants.
39 And this know, that if the goodman of the house had known what hour the thief would come, he would have watched, and not have suffered his house to be broken through.
40 Be ye therefore ready also: for the Son of man cometh at an hour when ye think not.
41 ¶ Then Peter said unto him, Lord, speakest thou this parable unto us, or even to all?
42 And the Lord said, Who then is that faithful and wise steward, whom *his* lord shall make ruler over his household, to give *them their* portion of meat in due season?
43 Blessed *is* that servant, whom his lord when he cometh shall find so doing.
44 Of a truth I say unto you, that he will make him ruler over all that he hath.
45 But and if that servant say in his heart, My lord delayeth his coming; and shall begin to beat the men servants and maidens, and to eat and drink, and to be drunken;
46 The lord of that servant will come in a day when he looketh not for *him*, and at an hour when he is not aware, and will cut him in sunder, and will appoint him his portion with the unbelievers.
47 And that servant, which knew his lord's will, and prepared not *himself*, neither did according to his will, shall be beaten with many *stripes*.
48 But he that knew not, and did commit things worthy of stripes, shall be beaten with few *stripes*. For unto whomsoever much is given, of him shall be much required; and to whom men have committed much, of him they will ask the more.

35. WHAT did the Lord tell his disciples?
To what custom in *dress* did he allude when he said, *Let your loins be girded about?* *

---

* See Biblical Antiquities, Part I., ch. 5, sec. 1.

How were the children of Israel commanded to eat the passover?—Ex. xii. 11.
Why were their loins girded, or their garments bound up? (That they might not hinder active exertion.)
What does our Lord mean when he tells his people to gird up their loins?—1 Pet. i. 13-15.
What ancient custom at weddings is alluded to in directing them to have their *lights burning?*—See next verse.

36. Whom should they themselves be like?
What was the duty of these men?
How does this apply to the duty of Christians? (They are to be always ready for the coming of the Lord.)
In what way may the Lord Jesus be said to come?—Rev. i. 18.
How can his people prepare to meet him?—1 John ii. 28.
What parable did our Lord speak, in which he alluded to this same custom?—See Matt. xxv. 1-12.
What happened to those who were not ready? (They were not admitted.)
When may the Lord be said to *come and knock?* (When he calls men to die.)
What have *you* to do that you may be ready to open to him *immediately?*

37. What servants did Jesus declare blessed?
What is meant here by *watching?* (Being prepared.)
In what way should those who love Christ watch for him?—Eph. vi. 18.
Do we know when our death or the judgment-day will come?
Should we not then be ready every moment?
How did Paul feel about dying?—2 Tim. iv. 6-8.
What will the bridegroom do who finds his servants watching?
How may this be applied to the manner in which Christ will receive his people? (He will receive them into heaven and make them happy there.)

38. What is said about the different times of the bridegroom's coming?
Into how many watches did the Jews divide the night? (Four.)
What is to be understood by the coming of the Lord Jesus in the *second watch,* or in the *third watch?* (He will come, but no one can tell the time.)
What was the message of the Lord Jesus to the Church in Sardis?—Rev. iii. 2, 3.

39. What other comparison did Jesus make?
Is the suddenness of the coming of Christ spoken of in this way in other places?—See 1 Thess. v. 2; 2 Pet. iii. 10.
What advice does the apostle Paul give to Christians on this account?—1 Thess. v. 6-8.

INSTRUCTIONS OF THE SAVIOUR.

What advice does the apostle Peter give?—2 Pet. iii. 11-14.

40. What did Christ himself say?
Are those ready who have not repented of their sins and believed in Christ? (No.—John iii. 18.)

41. What did Peter then say to Jesus?
Whom did he mean by *us?* (The apostles.)
Whom did he mean by *all?* (All Christians.)

42. How did the Lord answer him?
What is a *steward?* (One who manages the affairs of another.)
How are Christians stewards of God?
What is their duty?—1 Pet. iv. 10.
How is this to be done? (By doing all the good we can; according to our abilities and possessions.)
What are ministers of the gospel especially called?—1 Cor. iv. 1.
What is the duty of such?—1 Cor. iv. 2.
What duty of stewards is mentioned in this verse?
How does this apply to ministers?—2 Tim. ii. 15.

43. What is said of the faithful servant?

44. What is the promise to him?

45. What other kind of servant is spoken of?
How does he act?
What is represented by these actions? (Cruelty and oppression.)
What is meant by "my lord *delayeth* his coming?"
Why would not this be an excuse for misconduct in a servant? (His duty was to obey his master, whether present or absent.)
Is it any excuse for sin that the day of death or judgment does not seem to be near? (No.)
What is often the case with men who think thus?—See Eccl. viii. 11.
What is the consequence of such conduct?—See Rom. ii. 5.
What effect ought the forbearance of God to have?—See Rom. ii. 5.

46. When will the Lord of the unfaithful servant come?
What will he do with him?
With whom shall his portion be appointed?
What is the portion of unbelievers?—Mark xvi. 16.
What is the expression in Matthew's Gospel?—Matt. xxiv. 51.

47. What servant shall be beaten with many stripes?
What is the meaning of that? (His punishment shall be very severe.)
How does this apply to those who know what the will of God is, but neither prepare themselves, nor do according to his will? (Their punishment will be the most dreadful.)

48. What is said of him that knew not and did commit things worthy of stripes?
What reason is given for this?
Why should those who know God's will, and do it not, be punished more severely than those who did not know it? (Their sin is greater, for they might have obeyed and did not.)
Are there any persons who have not the means of knowing what is right and wrong?—See Rom. i. 19, 20.
Is any one living in a Christian land excusable for not knowing his Master's will? (Any one who has neglected an opportunity of knowing it is inexcusable.)
What does the word of God say of all men?—Rom. iii. 23.
What are *things worthy of stripes?* (What deserve punishment.)

LESSON XXII.

Christ warns the people to enter in at the strait gate and laments over Jerusalem.

LUKE xiii. 23-35.

23 Then said one unto him, Lord, are there few that be saved? And he said unto them,

24 ¶ Strive to enter in at the strait gate: for many, I say unto you, will seek to enter in, and shall not be able.

25 When once the master of the house is risen up, and hath shut to the door, and ye begin to stand without, and to knock at the door, saying, Lord, Lord, open unto us; and he shall answer and say unto you, I know you not whence ye are:

26 Then shall ye begin to say, We have eaten and drunk in thy presence, and thou hast taught in our streets.

27 But he shall say, I tell you, I know you not whence ye are; depart from me, all *ye* workers of iniquity.

28 There shall be weeping and gnashing of teeth, when ye shall see Abraham, and Isaac, and Jacob, and all the prophets, in the kingdom of God, and you *yourselves* thrust out.

29 And they shall come from the east, and *from* the west, and from the north, and *from* the south, and shall sit down in the kingdom of God.

30 And, behold, there are last which shall be first; and there are first which shall be last.

31 ¶ The same day there came certain of the Pharisees, saying unto him, Get thee out, and depart hence: for Herod will kill thee.

32 And he said unto them, Go ye, and tell that fox, Behold, I cast out devils, and I do cures to-day and to-morrow, and the third *day* I shall be perfected.

33 Nevertheless I must walk to-day, and to-morrow, and the *day* following: for it cannot be that a prophet perish out of Jerusalem.

34 O Jerusalem, Jerusalem, which killest the prophets, and stonest them that are sent unto thee; how often would I have gathered thy children together, as a hen *doth gather* her brood under *her* wings, and ye would not!

35 Behold, your house is left unto you desolate: and verily I say unto you, Ye shall not see me until *the time* come when ye shall say, Blessed *is* he that cometh in the name of the Lord.

23. WHAT did one say to Jesus?

INSTRUCTIONS OF THE SAVIOUR. 69

What is it to be *saved?* (To have eternal life.)
Is it right to inquire about subjects which God has chosen not to reveal? (No.)
What did Moses say on this subject?—Deut. xxix. 29.

24. How did Jesus answer the question?
How did this reprove the man who asked the question? (It showed him that the important question was, How to be saved.)
What did Christ exhort the people to do?
What is it to *strive?* (To endeavour earnestly.)
What is the meaning of *strait* here? (Narrow.)
What is meant by the strait gate? (The entrance to the way to heaven.)
Why is the way to heaven called strait?—See Matt. vii. 13, 14.
Why must we strive to enter in? (Because there is so much to oppose us.)
What will many do?
What sort of persons will not be able to enter in?—See Matt. vii. 22, 23. Rev. xxi. 27.
Who else will not be able to enter in?—Prov. i. 24–29.
How is the door of mercy shut on sinners? (By death.)

25. *When* shall some seek and not be able to enter in?
Who is meant by the *master of the house?* (Jesus.)
After the door is shut, what shall they begin to do?
What shall he answer?
Why will such be sent away by Christ?—See Matt. vii. 21.
Has not the Lord Jesus said, *Knock, and it shall be opened?* (Yes.)
But what did he say to Jerusalem?—Luke xix. 42.
What does this teach us about the danger of putting off applying to Christ? (We do not know how soon death may come and close the door of mercy on us.)

26. What shall they then begin to say?
How can sinners say this? (They can profess to be the friends of Christ.)
What privileges have you had which are like this?
Will they be of any advantage if you neglect them?
How does this apply to those who have professed to be the disciples of Christ, but are not? (Their profession will not save them.)

27. But what shall the master of the house answer?
Does not the Lord *know* all the creatures he has made?—Acts xv. 18.
What sort of knowledge does he mean here? (Friendship, approbation.)
Who are *workers of iniquity?* (The wicked.)
What is written in Psalm v. 4, 5?

28. How shall those feel who are sent away from Christ?
What will they see?
What is expressed by *gnashing of teeth?* (Anguish.)
Who were Abraham, Isaac, and Jacob? (The founders of the Jewish nation.)
What made this very forcible to the mind of the Jews? (They were the descendants of these Patriarchs.)
What is meant *here* by the kingdom of God? (Heaven.)
Why shall they be thrust out?—Ps. lxxviii. 22.
On what occasion did our Lord say this?—See Matt. viii. 5–13.
Was that centurion a Jew or a Gentile? (A Gentile.)
How will those feel who will see all the holy men they have read of in the Bible received into heaven, and themselves shall be thrust out?
How will those feel who shall see their pious relations separated from them in this manner.

29. From whence shall they come, who shall sit down in the kingdom of God?

30. What did our Lord then say?
How did he explain the meaning of this saying?—See Matt. xx. 1–16.
How would it apply to the calling of the Gentiles?—See Acts xiii. 45, 46.
How will it apply to all who have great privileges which they neglect? (Neglected privileges will intensify their punishment.)

31. Who came to Jesus that day?
What did they say to him?
Who was Herod?—See Luke iii. 1.
Where then must Christ have been at this time? (In Galilee.)
Where was he going?—See ver. 22.
Why would Herod wish to kill Jesus? (He feared his influence.)
Whom had he already killed?—See Matt. xiv. 3, 10.

32. What did Jesus answer?
Why did he call Herod a fox? (For his artful endeavour to send Jesus away.)
Was he afraid to stay in Galilee?
What did he mean to let Herod know by saying he should do cures to-day and to-morrow? (He would not discontinue his work because of Herod's threats.)
What did he mean by being *perfected?* (His work in Galilee would be completed.)
Could either the Jews or Romans take his life before the time appointed by God? (No.)

33. What did he say he must do?

Why must he so do?
What did our Lord mean by saying that? (Many prophets had been slain at Jerusalem and Jesus knew that he was to die there.)

34. How did he speak of Jerusalem?
Why were the prophets and messengers sent by God to Jerusalem?—Jer. xliv. 4.
Why did they stone and kill them? (The prophets reproved their sins.)
To what did the Lord compare his care of Jerusalem?
For what purpose does a hen gather her brood under her wings? (For their protection.)
Why were the Jews *not* gathered and protected thus by the Lord?
What did the Lord Jesus say to them on another occasion?—John v. 40.

35. What did Jesus say of them?
What is meant by their *house?* (The temple.)
What is the meaning of *desolate?* (Destroyed.)
When and how did these words of our Lord come to pass? (It was burned when Jerusalem was destroyed by the Romans, A. D. 70.)
What did he farther tell them in this verse?
Where was that said?—Luke xix. 37, 38.

LESSON XXIII.

The Parable of the Great Supper.

LUKE xiv. 16-33.

16 Then said he unto him, A certain man made a great supper, and bade many:
17 And sent his servant at supper time to say to them that were bidden, Come: for all things are now ready.
18 And they all with one *consent* began to make excuse. The first said unto him, I have bought a piece of ground, and I must needs go and see it: I pray thee have me excused.
19 And another said, I have bought five yoke of oxen, and I must go to prove them: I pray thee have me excused.

20 And another said, I have married a wife, and therefore I cannot come.
21 So that servant came, and shewed his lord these things. Then the master of the house, being angry, said to his servant, Go out quickly into the streets and lanes of the city, and bring in hither the poor, and the maimed, and the halt, and the blind.
22 And the servant said, Lord, it is done as thou hast commanded, and yet there is room.
23 And the Lord said unto the servant, Go out into the highways and

72 PARABLES AND OTHER

hedges and compel *them* to come in, that my house may be filled.

24 For I say unto you, That none of those men which were bidden shall taste of my supper.

25 ¶ And there went great multitudes with him: and he turned, and said unto them,

26 If any *man* come to me, and hate not his father, and mother, and wife, and children, and brethren, and sisters, yea, and his own life also, he cannot be my disciple.

27 And whosoever doth not bear his cross, and come after me, cannot be my disciple.

28 For which of you, intending to build a tower, sitteth not down first, and counteth the cost, whether he have *sufficient* to finish *it?*

29 Lest haply, after he hath laid the foundation, and is not able to finish *it,* all that behold *it* begin to mock him,

30 Saying, This man began to build, and was not able to finish.

31 Or what king, going to make war against another king, sitteth not down first, and consulteth whether he be able with ten thousand to meet him that cometh against him with twenty thousand?

32 Or else, while the other is yet a great way off, he sendeth an ambassage, and desireth conditions of peace.

33 So likewise, whosoever he be of you that forsaketh not all that he hath, he cannot be my disciple.

16. WHAT parable is recorded here?
How came our Lord to speak it?—See ver. 15.
How does it begin?
Whom did our Lord mean to represent by this man? (God.)
What is meant by the *great supper?* (The Gospel.)
Why is the Gospel like a great supper? (It provides salvation for the souls of men.)
How are *many bidden* to this supper? (Salvation is offered to them.)
What invitation do you find written in Isaiah lv. 1?
What people did the Lord first call to partake of his salvation? (The Jews.)

17. To whom did the man send his servant?
What is represented by the man sending his servant to call them? (God sending his servants to proclaim the Gospel.)
What servants has God sent to call on men to come to him? (Those who preach the Gospel.)
What was the servant to say?
How does this apply to the calling of sinners? (Jesus has made the atonement, sinners have only to accept it.)

18. How did those who were invited treat the invitation?
What did the first say?
What excuse like this do sinners often make? (That they have not time just now.)
What did Christ compare them to?—Matt. xiii. 22.

19. What did another say?
What is meant by proving them? (Trying them.)
Is there any thing of so much importance as to excuse us for neglecting the Gospel? (No.—Luke x. 41, 42.)

20. What did another do?

INSTRUCTIONS OF THE SAVIOUR. 73

How does the love of friends keep persons from attending to the Gospel? (When they love them more than God.)
What has Christ said of such?—Matt. x. 37.

21. What did the servant do when they all refused?
How was the master of the house affected?
What did he say to his servant?
How does this apply to the rejection of the Jews and the calling of the Gentiles? (The Gospel was offered first to the Jews, and after they refused it, to the Gentiles.)
How may it be applied to the manner in which the rich and worldly, and the poor and afflicted, treat the Gospel?

22. Did these come?
Was there room for more?

23. What did the Lord then bid his servant do?
What are *highways* and *hedges?* (Highways are public roads; hedges, fences of thorny bushes.)
Whom was he to compel to come in? (Those whom he found there.)
What is meant by *compel them to come in?* (It means here to urge earnestly.)
How does the apostle Paul direct Timothy to act?—2 Tim. iv. 2.
How did he himself speak to the Corinthians?—2 Cor. v. 20.

24. What did the Lord say of those who were bidden?
Who are represented by those who were bidden? (The Jews.)
What is written concerning the Jews in Acts xiii. 46?
How will this prove true of all who excuse themselves, and refuse to come to God?—Prov. i. 24-28.
What will be the doom of the finally impenitent?—Luke xiii. 28.

25. Who went with Jesus?

26. What did he say to them?
What is meant here by hating our near relations, and even our own lives, for Christ's sake? (Loving Christ more than we do them.)
How does our Lord express it in Matthew x. 37?
What are the words of the apostle Paul in Acts xx. 24; and xxi. 13; and Phil. iii. 8?
What is it to be Christ's disciple? (To love and obey him always,—to learn his will.)

27. What else did our Lord say on this subject?
What is meant by *bearing the cross?* (Taking cheerfully any sacrifice or self-denial which the service of Christ requires.)
Is it ever a disgrace in the opinion of the world to be an humble Christian?—Ps. cxix. 51.
How may men show that they are ashamed of the cross of Christ?. (By refusing to confess him.)
What is it to come after Christ?—John xv. 14.

What comfort have the disciples of Jesus under all these hardships?—John xvi. 33.

28. What question did Jesus ask?
What is a tower? (A strong, high building.)
What is meant by his counting the cost? (Calculating the expense.)

29. Why should a man count the cost first?

30. What would they say?
How does this apply to persons who wish to be Christians? (They should give the subject serious thought.)
What should such first consider? (If they are willing to persevere through trials and difficulties.)

31, 32. What other case did Jesus mention?
What does this teach us?—Heb. x. 38.
If it alludes to the opposition of the wicked to Christ, how may it be explained?—Ps. 2.

33. What is the great lesson taught by these examples?
What self-denials must you expect if you would be the disciple of Christ?
Why should you prefer him to your life, and to all your relatives?—John xv. 13.
What is said in Romans xiv. 8?
What promise is made to him who gives up all for Christ?—Matt. xix. 29.

LESSON XXIV.

Parable of the Prodigal Son.

LUKE xv. 11–32.

11 ¶ And he said, A certain man had two sons:

12 And the younger of them said to *his* father, Father, give me the portion of goods that falleth *to me.* And he divided unto them *his* living.

13 And not many days after, the younger son gathered all together, and took his journey into a far country, and there wasted his substance with riotous living.

14 And when he had spent all, there arose a mighty famine in that land; and he began to be in want.

15 And he went and joined himself to a citizen of that country; and he sent him into his field to feed swine.

16 And he would fain have filled his belly with the husks that the swine did eat: and no man gave unto him.

17 And when he came to himself, he said, How many hired servants of my father's have bread enough and to spare, and I perish with hunger!

18 I will arise and go to my father, and will say unto him, Father, I have sinned against heaven, and before thee,

19 And am no more worthy to be called thy son: make me as one of thy hired servants.

20 And he arose, and came to his father. But when he was yet a great way off, his father saw him, and had

INSTRUCTIONS OF THE SAVIOUR.

compassion, and ran, and fell on his neck, and kissed him.

21 And the son said unto him, Father, I have sinned against heaven, and in thy sight, and am no more worthy to be called thy son.

22 But the father said to his servants, Bring forth the best robe, and put it on him; and put a ring on his hand, and shoes on his feet:

23 And bring hither the fatted calf, and kill it; and let us eat, and be merry:

24 For this my son was dead, and is alive again; he was lost, and is found. And they began to be merry.

25 Now his elder son was in the field: and as he came and drew nigh to the house, he heard music and dancing.

26 And he called one of the servants, and asked what these things meant.

27 And he said unto him, Thy brother is come; and thy father hath killed the fatted calf, because he hath received him safe and sound.

28 And he was angry, and would not go in: therefore came his father out, and entreated him.

29 And he answering said to his father, Lo, these many years do I serve thee, neither transgressed I at any time thy commandment: and yet thou never gavest me a kid, that I might make merry with my friends:

30 But as soon as this thy son was come, which hath devoured thy living with harlots, thou hast killed for him the fatted calf.

31 And he said unto him, Son, thou art ever with me, and all that I have is thine.

32 It was meet that we should make merry, and be glad: for this thy brother was dead, and is alive again; and was lost, and is found.

11. WHAT parable is related in this passage?
Why is this commonly called the parable of the *prodigal* son? (It is the account of a young man who spent his property and ruined himself by his vices.)
On what occasion did Christ speak it?—See ver. 1, 2.
How does it begin?

12. What did the younger son ask?
What did the father do?

13. What did the younger son do?
Where did he go?
What did he do there?
What is meant by his *substance?* (His property.)
What is *riotous living?* (Dissipation.)
Repeat Eccl. xi. 9.

14. When he had spent all, what happened?
And what was his case then?

15. What did he do then?
What is meant by *joining himself?* (Became his servant.)
How was he employed?

16. How did he suffer with hunger?
What is supposed to be meant by *husks?* *
Did any one pity him?

17. When he came to himself, what did he say?

---

* See Bible Dictionary.

What is meant by his coming to himself? (He was restored to his right mind.)

18. What did he determine to do?
What did he resolve to say to his father?
What did he mean by saying, *I have sinned against heaven?* (That he had sinned against God.)
Against whom is all sin committed? (Against God.)
How?—Jer. ix. 13.
What did David say when weeping over his sins?—Ps. li. 4.
Then if *you* are really sorry for sin, what will be your greatest grief?

19. What did the prodigal say of his unworthiness?
What would he desire his father to make him?

20. What did he do?
What took place?
How is this like the conduct of God towards repenting sinners?—Neh. ix. 17, last clause.

21. What did the son say to him?

22. What did the father say to his servants?
Were these articles worn by men in ancient times?—Gen. xli. 42; Esther viii. 2.
How does God treat penitent sinners?—Isa. lv. 7.

23. What else did the father order to be done?

24. Why were all these things to be done?
How had his son been dead and was alive again? (He had been dead to all good, but was restored.)
How may a sinner be said to be dead?—Eph. ii. 1.
When is he alive again?—Rom. vi. 11.
Can you remember any passage of Scripture which represents sinners as *lost?*—Luke xix. 10; Matt. xv. 24.
What may the gladness of the household represent?—Ver. 10.
Why do you suppose the angels and saints of God rejoice over a returning sinner? (Because it is life from the dead.)

25. Where was the elder son?
What is said of him?
Who are probably represented by the elder and younger sons? (The Pharisees by the elder; penitent sinners by the younger.)
Why may the Jews be called the elder children of God? (They were first chosen as God's peculiar people.)
Why may the Gentiles be called the younger? (The gospel was given to the Gentiles as well as Jews.)

26. What did he inquire of one of the servants?

27. What did the servant say to him?

28. How did he behave when he heard this?

Whose conduct is represented here?—Ver. 2.
What did his father do?

29. How did the elder son answer his father?
What is represented as the spirit of the Pharisees, in Luke xviii. 11, 12?
What does the apostle Paul say of the Jews in Rom. x. 3?
Will a real servant of God think that he deserves to be rewarded for what he does? (Never.)
What does the Lord teach his people in Luke xvii. 10?

30. What did the elder son say of his brother?
How should he have felt towards his penitent brother? (He should have rejoiced in his return.)

31. How did his father answer him?
What did he mean by saying, *thou art ever with me?* (He had never left him.)
Did his father take any thing from him to give to his brother? (No.)
What did the Lord say to Cain when he was angry with his brother?—Gen. iv. 6, 7.

32. What more did his father say?
What is the meaning of, *it was meet?* (It was proper.)
Why was it meet?
What warning does this parable hold out to those who leave the Lord, and walk in their own ways?—Jer. xiii. 16.
What encouragement to returning sinners? (God will receive them graciously, as this father received his son.)
How does it show the readiness of God to pardon sin? (This father forgave willingly, and so God is not willing that any should perish.)
What did the younger son do before his father had pity on him?—Ver. 18, 19.
What do you learn from that?

LESSON XXV.

Parable of the Unjust Steward.

Luke xvi. 1-17.

1 And he said also unto his disciples, There was a certain rich man, which had a steward; and the same was accused unto him that he had wasted his goods.

2 And he called him, and said unto him, How is it that I hear this of thee? give an account of thy stewardship; for thou mayest be no longer steward.

3 Then the steward said within him-

self, What shall I do? for my lord taketh away from me the stewardship: I cannot dig; to beg I am ashamed.
4 I am resolved what to do, that, when I am put out of the stewardship, they may receive me into their houses.
5 So he called every one of his lord's debtors *unto him*, and said unto the first, How much owest thou unto my lord?
6 And he said, An hundred measures of oil. And he said unto him, Take thy bill, and sit down quickly, and write fifty.
7 Then said he to another, And how much owest thou? And he said, An hundred measures of wheat. And he said unto him, Take thy bill, and write fourscore.
8 And the lord commended the unjust steward, because he had done wisely: for the children of this world are in their generation wiser than the children of light.
9 And I say unto you, Make to yourselves friends of the mammon of unrighteousness; that, when ye fail, they may receive you into everlasting habitations.
10 He that is faithful in that which is least is faithful also in much: and he that is unjust in the least is unjust also in much.
11 If therefore ye have not been faithful in the unrighteous mammon, who will commit to your trust the true riches?
12 And if ye have not been faithful in that which is another man's, who shall give you that which is your own?
13 ¶ No servant can serve two masters: for either he will hate the one, and love the other; or else he will hold to the one, and despise the other. Ye cannot serve God and mammon.
14 And the Pharisees also, who were covetous, heard all these things: and they derided him.
15 And he said unto them, Ye are they which justify yourselves before men; but God knoweth your hearts: for that which is highly esteemed among men is abomination in the sight of God.
16 The law and the prophets *were* until John: since that time the kingdom of God is preached, and every man presseth into it.
17 And it is easier for heaven and earth to pass, than one tittle of the law to fail.

1. To whom did Jesus speak this parable?
What did he say of a certain rich man?
What is a steward? (One who has charge of another person's affairs.)
Of what was the steward accused?

2. What did the rich man do when he heard this?
What was it to give an account of his stewardship? (To make a statement of the affairs.)

3. What did the steward say within himself?
What is meant by saying he *could not dig?* (He was unwilling to work.)

4. What else did he say?

5. What did he do?
What are debtors? (Those who owe any thing.)
What did he say to the first?

6. What did the debtor answer?
What did the steward say to him?
How could the steward profit by this? (He supposed they would repay the obligation by giving him a support.)

7. What did he say to another?

INSTRUCTIONS OF THE SAVIOUR.

What did the man say?
What did the steward say to him?
How many are *fourscore?* (Eighty.)
How would he make friends by this conduct? (He released them from part of their debts.)

8. Why did the steward's master commend the unjust steward?
Why is he called unjust? (He defrauded his master.)
How had he done wisely? (He had secured the friendship of the debtors.)
What was it in the conduct of the steward that his master commended? (His prudence.)
For what purpose had he done it?—Verse 4.
Did his master say he had done *right?* (No.)
What did Jesus say of the children of this world?
Who are they? (Those who live for this world.—2 Cor. iv. 4.)
Who are meant by the children of light? (Christians.—1 Thess. v. 5.)
In what respect are the children of this world often wiser in worldly plans than Christians are in doing good? (In the activity and interest with which they pursue them.)
Do those who have light and knowledge always prepare for the future world?—John vii. 48.
What was this wicked steward anxious to secure? (His future maintenance.)
If he was so careful to provide for this life, how ought you to provide for eternity?

9. What other lesson did Jesus teach from this?
What is meant by the mammon of unrighteousness? (Riches.)
How are the Lord's people to make to themselves friends by riches?—1 Tim. vi. 17-19.
What directions does Jesus give his people in Luke xii. 33?
What reward is promised to such?
What is meant here by *failing?* (Dying.)
How must we use our property if we expect to reach heaven? (As being the Lord's stewards.)

10. What does Jesus say of him that is faithful in that which is least?
What is meant by being faithful in that which is least? (Faithful in small matters.)
What example have we of one who was faithful in little?—Mark xii. 41-44.
What is said of him who is unjust in the least?
What is it to be unjust in the least? (Unjust in little things.)
Why would such a one be unjust in greater things? (The same disposition would govern him.)

PARABLES AND OTHER

11. What question does Jesus ask here?
What is it to be faithful in the unrighteous mammon?—2 Cor. ix. 9.
What are the *true riches?* (The blessings of God.)
Why are the blessings of God true riches? (They are satisfying and lasting.)
What is said in the Bible on this point?—See Prov. x. 22; Matt. vi. 20.

12. What other question did Jesus ask?
If you are unfaithful to the trust God commits to you in this world, can you expect him to give you the heavenly treasure?

13. What does Jesus say no servant can do?
What two masters does the Lord say you cannot serve?
What is meant here by *mammon?* (Earthly riches.)
Why cannot one serve God and mammon?
What is written concerning this in 1 John ii. 15, 16?
When had Jesus said this before?—See Matt. vi. 24.
What advice did he then give to his disciples?—Matt vi. 19-21, 33.
Suppose a man serves the world faithfully, and the hour of death comes, what can the world do for him?—Ps. xlix. 17.
But what promise has the faithful servant of God?—Matt. xxv. 21.
To whom shall we give an account of the use which we make of the things of this world?—Rom. xiv. 12.
Do we know how soon we shall be dismissed from our stewardship?

14. Who were offended at these sayings?
Why were they offended?
How did they treat Christ?
What is it to deride? (To ridicule.)

15. What did Jesus say to them?
Could they deceive God?
How differently may the same things appear to God and to men?
What things are here meant? (Those things which are done not to please God, but to appear well to men.)
How did this apply to the Pharisees?—Matt. xxiii. 2-5.

16. What else did Jesus say?
What John is here meant?—Matt. xi. 12, 13.
What change then took place?
What is the kingdom here spoken of? (The Gospel dispensation.)

17. Did the law cease to be in force when John came?
What then did Christ mean by saying that the law and the

INSTRUCTIONS OF THE SAVIOUR. 81

prophets *were until John?* (The Old Testament dispensation closed when John came.)
How must sinners *press* into the kingdom of Christ? (They must seek it earnestly.)

LESSON XXVI.

Parable of the Rich Man and Lazarus.

On what subject had Christ instructed the people in this chapter?—(Ver. 1–17.)

LUKE xvi. 19–31.

19 ¶ There was a certain rich man, which was clothed in purple and fine linen, and fared sumptuously every day:
20 And there was a certain beggar named Lazarus, which was laid at his gate, full of sores.
21 And desiring to be fed with the crumbs which fell from the rich man's table: moreover the dogs came and licked his sores,
22 And it came to pass, that the beggar died, and was carried by the angels into Abraham's bosom: the rich man also died, and was buried;
23 And in hell he lift up his eyes, being in torments, and seeth Abraham afar off, and Lazarus in his bosom.
24 And he cried and said, Father Abraham, have mercy on me, and send Lazarus, that he may dip the tip of his finger in water, and cool my tongue; for I am tormented in this flame.
25 But Abraham said, Son, remember that thou in thy lifetime receivedst thy good things, and likewise Lazarus evil things: but now he is comforted, and thou art tormented.
26 And besides all this, between us and you there is a great gulf fixed; so that they which would pass from hence to you cannot; neither can they pass to us, that *would come* from thence.
27 Then he said, I pray thee therefore, father, that thou wouldest send him to my father's house:
28 For I have five brethren; that he may testify unto them, lest they also come into this place of torment.
29 Abraham saith unto him, They have Moses and the prophets; let them hear them.
30 And he said, Nay, father Abraham: but if one went unto them from the dead, they will repent.
31 And he said unto him, If they hear not Moses and the prophets, neither will they be persuaded, though one rose from the dead.

19. What did he afterwards tell them?
What is signified by his being clothed in purple?*
What is the meaning of *fared sumptuously?* (Lived luxuriously.)
20. What other person is mentioned in this parable?
Where was he laid?
What was his condition?
What do we understand by his *being laid* at the gate? (He was placed their to excite pity and obtain aid.)
Was there any public provision made for the poor in those days? (No.)

---

* See Biblical Antiquities, Part I., chap. 5, sec. 1.

21. What else is said of his poverty?
22. What became of the beggar?
What became of him *after* death?
What then must his character have been? (Righteous.)
What do we learn about the angels in Heb. i. 14?
What is meant by Abraham's bosom? (Being with Abraham in heaven.)
To what custom is there an allusion here?—See John xiii. 23.
Who was Abraham, and what was his character?—Gen. xii. 1, 2; James ii. 23.
What may you learn from the care of angels over the soul of a poor beggar?—1 Sam. xvi. 7.
What is said of the rich man?
23. Where was the rich man after death?
What then was his character? (He was worldly; he had laid up his treasures on earth.)
What proof does this account give that the wicked will go into torments? (This wicked man was in torment.)
Whom did the rich man see?
Who was with Abraham?
24. What did the rich man cry out?
Why did the Jews call Abraham *father?* (They were his descendants.)
How is the distress of this man represented?
How did Christ commonly speak of the punishment of the wicked?—See Matt. xxv. 41.
What sort of people will be sent to this punishment?—Ps. ix. 17.
Is it not dreadful to think of being with such persons forever?
25. How did Abraham answer the rich man?
What were the good things that the rich man received in his lifetime? (Wealth, and the pleasures of this life.)
Was the rich man punished *because* he was rich? (No.)
Why then? (Because he had loved those riches and not God.)
What evil things had Lazarus received? (Poverty and affliction.)
Was Lazarus taken to heaven because he was poor and afflicted? (No.)
Why then? (Because he had loved and trusted in God.)
In what must the poor of this world be rich, to be heirs of the kingdom?—James ii. 5.
If you seek to have your portion in the good things of this life, what may you expect in the life to come?
What state is most favourable to piety—riches, or poverty?
What is the prayer of Agur in Prov. xxx. 8?
26. What did Abraham say farther?
What is a *gulf?* (A chasm.)

INSTRUCTIONS OF THE SAVIOUR. 83

What is meant by its being *fixed?* (Permanently placed.)
What does this mean? (The eternal separation of the righteous and wicked.)
What did he say about passing it?
Then is there any hope for those who are in hell of getting to heaven at last? (No.—Rev. xxi. 27.)
Repeat 2 Thess. i. 9.

27. What did the rich man then pray Abraham to do?
Send *whom?*—Verse 24.

28. Why did he wish Lazarus to be sent to his family?
What is the meaning of *testify?* (Bear witness.)
What was Lazarus to testify? (The awful consequences of leading such lives.)
Why did he think this would keep them from that place? (He thought fear of the punishment would induce them to reform.)

29. What did Abraham say to him?
What did he mean by Moses and the prophets? (The Scriptures.)
How should they hear them? (Attend to them.)
How could attention to them keep them from hell?—Ps. cxix. 9; John v. 39.
What did Moses command them?—Deut. vi. 5.
What did the apostle say to Timothy about the Scriptures?—2 Tim. iii. 15.
What have you besides Moses and the prophets?
Will you not then be less excusable than the Jews, if you neglect your opportunities?

30. What did the rich man again say?
Are not people apt to think that if a spirit or angel were to speak to them, they would believe?
What is the true cause of unbelief?—John v. 40.

31. How did Abraham answer this?
Is not the testimony of God by his prophets more worthy of credit, than that of a person who should come from the invisible world? (Yes.—2 Pet. i. 21.)
What effect ought this account of the rich man and Lazarus to have upon sinners?—Jer. xxvi. 13.
If we desire the conversion and salvation of our friends, what is our duty to them while we are alive?
Will it be too late to lament, after death has taken us, or them, away?

LESSON XXVII.

Jesus teaches his people to forgive one another, and shows the power of faith.

LUKE xvii. 1–10.

1 Then said he unto the disciples, It is impossible but that offences will come: but woe *unto him*, through whom they come!
2 It were better for him that a millstone were hanged about his neck, and he cast into the sea, than that he should offend one of these little ones.
3 ¶ Take heed to yourselves: If thy brother trespass against thee, rebuke him; and if he repent, forgive him.
4 And if he trespass against thee seven times in a day, and seven times in a day turn again to thee, saying, I repent; thou shalt forgive him.
5 And the apostles said unto the Lord, Increase our faith.
6 And the Lord said, If ye had faith as a grain of mustard seed, ye might say unto this sycamine tree, Be thou plucked up by the root, and be thou planted in the sea; and it should obey you.
7 But which of you, having a servant ploughing or feeding cattle, will say unto him by and by, when he is come from the field, Go and sit down to meat?
8 And will not rather say unto him, Make ready wherewith I may sup, and gird thyself, and serve me, till I have eaten and drunken; and afterward thou shalt eat and drink?
9 Doth he thank that servant because he did the things that were commanded him? I trow not.
10 So likewise ye, when ye shall have done all those things which are commanded you, say, We are unprofitable servants: we have done that which was our duty to do.

1. WHAT did Jesus say to the disciples about offences?
What is meant by *offences* in this place? (Acts which occasion sin.)
What does the word mean in Matt. v. 29, &c.?
How did Christ apply it?—See next verse.
What is said of him through whom they come?
What did the apostle say?—Rom. xiv. 13.

2. What then did our Lord say?
Who are meant by *these little ones?* (Christians.)
On what occasion did Jesus say this?—See Matt. xviii.
What does the apostle Paul say in 1 Cor. viii. 12, 13?
How does a Christian *offend* his fellow Christians? (When one falls into sin through the other's wrong doing.)
Why are the sins of Christ's people so much to be dreaded?—Rom. ii. 23, 24.

3. What does the Lord here warn his disciples to do?
What is it to *take heed to yourself?* (Be very careful.)
What was a disciple told to do, if a brother trespassed against him?
What is it to trespass against a brother? (To injure him.)
What is it to *rebuke* a person? (To reprove.)
What is written in the law of God concerning this?—Lev. xix. 17.

INSTRUCTIONS OF THE SAVIOUR.

If thy brother repent, what is to be done?
In what manner must a Christian be rebuked?—Gal. vi. 1, and 2 Thess. iii. 15.
If you know the faults of a person, to whom should you first tell them?—Matt. xviii. 15.
How should you act when others tell you of *your* faults?
How did David think of this?—Ps. cxli. 5.

4. What does the Lord say farther of the duty of forgiveness?
Suppose that a person is not sorry for having offended you, may you then be unforgiving?
What is the command of Christ?—Matt. v. 44.

5. What did the apostles ask of the Lord?
Who were the apostles?—Luke vi. 13-16.
Why are they called apostles? (Apostle means one sent forth, and these Jesus sent forth first to preach the Gospel.)
What is faith? (Belief.)
Why is faith necessary to keep the commandments of Christ? (Christ gives the strength to those who believe on him.)
Can we perform this duty of forgiveness, or *any* duty, without faith? (Of ourselves we cannot do any good thing.)
If Jesus was but a mere prophet, and not God, would the apostles have asked this of him? (No; none but God has such power.)
Who is the Author of faith?—Heb. xii. 2.
When God's people have a hard duty to perform, how shall they get strength to perform it?—2 Cor. xii. 9; John xiv. 14.
What was Paul's experience?—Phil. iv. 13.
What is the importance of faith?—Heb. xi. 6.

6. How did the Lord answer the apostles?
What is meant by having faith as a grain of mustard-seed? (The least degree.)
What is meant by this comparison? (To show what difficult things a Christian can do through Christ strengthening him.)
What must be the nature of the things we ask from God in faith?—1 John v. 14.
In what chapter of the epistle to the Hebrews do you find an enumeration of the mighty works done through *faith?* (The eleventh.)
Can you mention any of them?
What is meant by true faith in Christ? (Believing and trusting in him alone for salvation.)

7. What did Jesus say next to his disciples?

8. What would the master say to his servant?

9. What question does he then ask?
How does Jesus himself answer it?

What is the meaning of *trow not?* (Think not.)
What is meant by saying that the master does not *thank* his servant? (He is not indebted to him.)

10. How does Jesus apply this to the disciples?
What is an *unprofitable servant?* (One who neglects his duties.)
Is it possible for us to do *more* than our duty to God? (No; we belong to him as our Creator.)
Has any one ever done *as much* as God has commanded him? (No.—Rom. iii. 23.)
Suppose you had kept all the commandments, would you deserve God's thanks for it?
Why not?
How then should you feel when you have been breaking them?
If a sinner repents, and does that which is right, is he entitled to any thanks? (No; it is God's free mercy that pardons him.)
Has he done any thing more than his duty? (No.)
What other reason can you give?—See John xv. 4, 5.

LESSON XXVIII.

The Parable of the Unjust Judge, and of the Pharisee and Publican.

LUKE xviii. 1-14.

1 And he spake a parable unto them to this end, that men ought always to pray, and not to faint;
2 Saying, There was in a city a judge, which feared not God, neither regarded man:
3 And there was a widow in that city; and she came unto him, saying, Avenge me of mine adversary.
4 And he would not for a while: but afterward he said within himself, Though I fear not God, nor regard man;
5 Yet because this widow troubleth me, I will avenge her, lest by her continual coming she weary me.
6 And the Lord said, Hear what the unjust judge saith.
7 And shall not God avenge his own elect, which cry day and night unto him, though he bear long with them?
8 I tell you that he will avenge them speedily. Nevertheless, when the Son of man cometh, shall he find faith on the earth?

9 And he spake this parable unto certain which trusted in themselves that they were righteous, and despised others:
10 Two men went up into the temple to pray; the one a Pharisee, and the other a publican.
11 The Pharisee stood and prayed thus with himself, God, I thank thee, that I am not as other men *are*, extortioners, unjust, adulterers, or even as this publican.
12 I fast twice in the week, I give tithes of all that I possess.
13 And the publican, standing afar off, would not lift up so much as *his* eyes unto heaven, but smote upon his breast, saying, God be merciful to me a sinner.
14 I tell you, this man went down to his house justified *rather* than the other; for every one that exalteth himself shall be abased; and he that humbleth himself shall be exalted.

INSTRUCTIONS OF THE SAVIOUR. 87

1. WHAT did Jesus again speak?
What did he mean to teach by it?
How can men *always* pray? (By keeping their hearts ready to ask God's blessing.)
Why do we *need* constant prayer? (Because we depend on God for every blessing.)
What is it to *faint?* (To grow weary.)

2. How did Jesus begin the parable?
What is a *judge?* (One who has authority to determine causes.)
What was the character of the judge?

3. Who came to him?
What did she ask?
What did she mean by this? (Do me justice.)
What directions did the Lord give his people of old respecting widows and fatherless children?—Ex. xxii. 22, 23.

4, 5. How did the judge act?
Why did he determine to attend to her case?

6. What did the Lord say?
If the judge attended to the widow's case, why is he called *unjust?*—See ver. 2.
Can we do things that are right from bad motives? (Yes.)
Will God be pleased with such conduct? (No; it is hypocritical conduct.)

7. What question did Jesus then ask concerning God's conduct to his people?
Who are meant by God's *own elect?* (Christians.)
Does the parable mean to teach that God answers the prayers of his people because they trouble him? (No.)
What is it meant to teach? (That God loves his people and will hear their prayers.)
How does much praying show that we really desire what we ask for? (We would not persevere if we did not desire it.)
How are God's people represented as crying to him?
What is meant by the words, *though he bear long with them?* (Though he delay to answer their prayers.)
Does the Lord always answer prayer immediately? (No.)
Why does he often seem not to hear his people? (To try their faith.)
Can you relate the account of the woman of Canaan, written in Matt. xv. 22-28?
What does David say in Ps. xxvii. 14?
Though the Lord leave his people to pray a long time, and they get no answer, what should they do?—Col. iv. 2.

8. When will the Lord avenge his people?

What question did Jesus ask?
What is the meaning of this? (Would his people believe that God is faithful and not cease to pray.)

9. To whom did Jesus then speak another parable?
What is there sinful in such a character? (It is proud and self-righteous.)
Why should every Christian be humble?—1 Cor. iv. 7.

10. Who are the two persons mentioned in the parable?
Who were the publicans? (Tax gatherers.)
Why were they generally despised by the Jews? (The Roman tax was very grievous to the Jews, and the collectors were often men of bad character.)
Who were the Pharisees? (A powerful sect, who claimed to possess extraordinary piety.)

11. How did the Pharisee pray?
What sort of heart does such a declaration show? (Proud.)

12. What did he boast of?
What is it to *fast?* (To abstain from food.)
What are *tithes?* (The tenth part.)
Were not fasting and giving tithes commanded by God? (Yes.)
How did the Pharisees and most of the Jews perform these duties, so as to make them displeasing to the Lord? (Ostentatiously, to secure the praise of men.)
What directions did Jesus give about fasting, in his sermon on the mount?—Matt. vi. 16-18.
What did the Lord Jesus say to the Pharisees about giving tithes, in Matt. xxiii. 23?
Why should we not take credit to ourselves, even for the *right* performance of *any* duty?—Phil. ii. 13; John xv. 5.

13. How did the publican pray?
Why did he stand afar off, and not lift up so much as his eyes to heaven? (He felt so unworthy.)
What is the meaning of *smote upon his breast?* (Struck upon it.)
What did this action signify? (Great sorrow.)
Can you tell how the prayer of the publican differed from that of the Pharisee?
What is the character of those whom God will hear?—See Isa. lxvi. 2.

14. What did Jesus say respecting the publican?
Why was he justified rather than the Pharisee? (God does not pardon sinners unless they are penitent.)
What is said by David that will apply to them?—Psalm cxxxviii. 6.

What is said of every one that exalteth himself?
What is the meaning of *abased?* (Humbled.)
What is said of him that humbleth himself?
How shall he be exalted?—Matt. v. 3.
What do you learn respecting prayer from the first of these parables? (That God will answer earnest prayer.)
What does the second parable teach you of the kind of prayer which is acceptable to God, and of the disposition with which it should be offered? (God accepts the sinner's prayer for mercy when it is offered with humility and faith.)
How does God regard those who have the spirit of the publican?—James iv. 6.
How is such a spirit to be obtained?—See Ps. li. 10.

LESSON XXIX.

Jesus blesses little children, and discourses with a rich man on eternal life.

MATT. xix. 13-24.

13 ¶ Then were there brought unto him little children, that he should put *his* hands on them, and pray: and the disciples rebuked them.
14 But Jesus said, Suffer little children, and forbid them not, to come unto me: for of such is the kingdom of heaven.
15 And he laid *his* hands on them, and departed thence.
16 ¶ And, behold, one came and said unto him, Good Master, what good thing shall I do, that I may have eternal life?
17 And he said unto him, Why callest thou me good? *there is* none good but one, *that is*, God: but if thou wilt enter into life, keep the commandments.
18 He saith unto him, Which? Jesus said, Thou shalt do no murder, Thou shalt not commit adultery, Thou shalt not steal, Thou shalt not bear false witness,

19 Honour thy father and *thy* mother: and, Thou shalt love thy neighbour as thyself.
20 The young man saith unto him, All these things have I kept from my youth up: what lack I yet?
21 Jesus said unto him, If thou wilt be perfect, go *and* sell that thou hast, and give to the poor, and thou shalt have treasure in heaven: and come *and* follow me.
22 But when the young man heard that saying, he went away sorrowful: for he had great possessions.
23 ¶ Then said Jesus unto his disciples, Verily I say unto you, That a rich man shall hardly enter into the kingdom of heaven.
24 And again I say unto you, It is easier for a camel to go through the eye of a needle, than for a rich man to enter into the kingdom of God.

13. Who were brought to Christ?
For what purpose were they brought?
What was signified by putting the hands on the head? (Blessing.)

What example is there of this in the Old Testament?—See Gen. xlviii. 9, 14, 16.
What do Mark and Luke call it?—Mark x. 13; Luke xviii. 15.
What did the disciples do?
What is the meaning of *rebuked?* (Reproved.)
Whom did the disciples rebuke?—See Mark x. 13.
Why, do you suppose, did they rebuke them? (They thought young children would not receive any benefit.)
How did Jesus feel when he saw this?—See Mark x. 14.

14. What did Jesus say to the disciples?
What did he say of the children?
What does that mean? (Such a character and temper prepares for heaven.)
How did Jesus explain it?—See Mark x. 15.
How again is this explained?—Matt. xviii. 3, 4.
What encouragement does the language of Christ give to children? (It shows them how willing the Saviour is to receive them.)
How can they go to Christ now? (By believing in him and praying to him.)
Why should they go whilst they are children?—Prov. viii. 17.

15. What did Jesus do then?
What is added in Mark x. 16?
How is the Lord represented in Isaiah xl. 11?

16. What did one who came to Jesus ask him?
Who was this person?—Luke xviii. 18.
How did he come?—Mark x. 17.
What is *eternal life?* (Eternal happiness in heaven.)

17. What did Jesus say to him?
Did Jesus mean to say that *he* was not God? (No.—John i. 1.)
What did he intend by saying so? (To teach them that such titles belong only to God.)
What did Jesus tell him to do?
Has any man ever kept the commandments so as to merit eternal life? (No.—Gal. ii. 16.)
But if any one expects to gain eternal life by his works, what must he do? (Keep the whole law perfectly; every "jot" and tittle.

18, 19. What did the young man ask him then?
What did Jesus say to him?
Are these all the commandments? (No.)
Why did Jesus only mention these? (It was these Jesus intended to convince him he had not kept.)

20. What did the young man say to Jesus?

INSTRUCTIONS OF THE SAVIOUR.

21. How did Jesus prove that this was not true?
If he loved his neighbour as himself, would he not have been willing to do as Jesus said? (Yes.)
How is this related by Mark?—Mark x. 21.
Would he have *deserved* eternal life by doing this? (No.—Eph. ii. 8.)
Was it not the best way of showing him that his heart must be changed first? (Yes.)
In what sense is it said by Mark that Jesus *loved* him? (Jesus loved what was amiable in his character.)

22. What did the young man do?
Why was he sorrowful?

23. What did Jesus say about it?
Did he say they cannot enter heaven? (No; he said that it was more difficult.)
Why is it more difficult for the rich than the poor to enter into heaven? (They have more temptations to pride, self-indulgence, and worldliness.)

24. What did Jesus again say to them?
What did the Lord mean by this? (That it was extremely difficult.)
How did Jesus explain this afterwards?—See ver. 26, and Mark x. 24.
Should we then desire what may be of such injury to us?
What was the *one thing* that this young man was destitute of? (A heart to love God more than his possessions.)
Is there not some one thing that keeps many from following Christ?
What does this lesson teach to those who are moral, but are not true Christians? (That they still lack the needful preparation for heaven.)

LESSON XXX.

Jesus teaches the Jews concerning Himself.

JOHN viii. 12-24.

12 ¶ Then spake Jesus again unto them, saying, I am the light of the world: he that followeth me shall not walk in darkness, but shall have the light of life.
13 The Pharisees therefore said unto him, Thou bearest record of thyself: thy record is not true.
14 Jesus answered and said unto them, Though I bear record of myself, yet my record is true: for I know whence I came, and whither I go; but ye cannot tell whence I come, and whither I go.
15 Ye judge after the flesh; I judge no man.
16 And yet if I judge, my judgment is true: for I am not alone, but I and the Father that sent me.
17 It is also written in your law, that the testimony of two men is true.
18 I am one that bear witness of myself, and the Father that sent me beareth witness of me.
19 Then said they unto him, Where is thy Father? Jesus answered, Ye neither know me, nor my Father: if ye had known me, ye should have known my Father also.
20 These words spake Jesus in the treasury, as he taught in the temple: and no man laid hands on him; for his hour was not yet come.
21 Then said Jesus again unto them, I go my way, and ye shall seek me, and shall die in your sins: whither I go, ye cannot come.
22 Then said the Jews, Will he kill himself? because he saith, Whither I go, ye cannot come.
23 And he said unto them, Ye are from beneath; I am from above: ye are of this world; I am not of this world.
24 I said therefore unto you, that ye shall die in your sins: for if ye believe not that I am he, ye shall die in your sins.

12. WHAT did Jesus say he was?
How is Jesus *the light of the world?* (He dispels the darkness of ignorance and sin.)
What kind of light did he bring into the world? (Spiritual.)
How does this light guide men?—Luke i. 79.
How should Christians imitate their Lord in this respect?— See Matt. v. 14-16.
What effect has this light on the impenitent?—See John iii. 19.
What effect ought it to have?—See John xii. 46.
What does Jesus promise the one that follows him?
What is it to *follow Christ?* (To follow his example.)
What is meant by *walking in darkness?* (Being ignorant and wicked.)
What is said of the path of the just, and of the way of the wicked?—Prov. iv. 18, 19.
How do those that follow Christ have this light? (His example is a perfect guide.)
What is meant by the *light of life?* (Spiritual light.)

13. What did the Pharisees say to Christ?
What is it *to bear record?* (To give testimony.)
How had Jesus just been bearing record of himself? (As being the light of the world.)

INSTRUCTIONS OF THE SAVIOUR.

Why would it not be considered a true record, if he bare it of himself? (Their law required two witnesses to substantiate a declaration.)

14. How did Jesus answer the Pharisees?
From whence had he come?—John iii. 13.
Whither was he going?—John xvi. 28.
What had he said before this?—See John v. 31.
Was his testimony the less true because the Jewish law would not admit it? (No.)
How does this explain the different meanings of Christ in the two places? (His testimony was not to be rejected, because no man could testify about things in heaven.)

15. How did Jesus tell the Pharisees they judged?
How did they judge after the flesh? (According to appearances.)
What judgment did they form of Jesus?—John ix. 22; Luke vii. 34.
When will be the time for Christ to judge all men?—Acts xvii. 31; Jude 14, 15.
What did he say of himself?

16. If he had judged, what would his judgment have been?
Why?
How was the Father with him?—John xiv. 11.

17. What was the Jewish law about testimony?
In what books of the Bible do you find the Jewish law? (The first five.)
Where do you find any thing respecting the testimony of two witnesses?—Deut. xix. 15.

18. Who were Christ's witnesses?
How did he bear witness of himself?—John v. 36.
How did the Father bear witness of him?—Matt. iii. 17.
What did Christ say to his disciples at another time?—See John xiv. 10.

19. What did the Pharisees then ask him?
How did Jesus answer them?
What is it to *know* God and Jesus Christ? (To believe in Jesus Christ as the Son of God.)
How did the Pharisees show that they did not know him? (They refused to believe in him as their Messiah.)
By what do people show that they know God?—1 John iv. 7.
What does the apostle Paul say of some who professed to know God?—Tit. i. 16.
How should they have known the Father if they had known Jesus?—See John x. 30.

20. Where did Jesus speak these words?
What was the treasury and where was it?*
What is remarked of the people?
What had Jesus said that was likely to provoke them to this? (That God was his Father.)
Why did they not do it?
What is meant by his *hour* not being yet come? (The time for his death had not come.)

21. What did Jesus again say to them?
Where was Jesus going?—John vii. 33.
What would be the consequence of dying in their sins?

22. What did the Jews then say?
Did they understand what he said? (Probably not.)

23. What did Jesus say to the Jews?
What did he mean by saying they were from beneath? (Their opinions were earthly, corrupt.)
What is meant by their being of this world? (Their thoughts and actions were governed by this world.)
How would these things prevent them from going to heaven? (They would prevent their believing in Christ.)

24. What did Jesus say again to them?
Why should they die in their sins?
Why was this so?—Acts iv. 12.
Is this true of the Jews only?—See John iii. 36.
What has Christ declared?—John iii. 16-18.
What is it really to believe in Christ? (To trust in him as our only and all-sufficient Saviour.)

LESSON XXXI.

Christ the Good Shepherd.

JOHN x. 1-18.

1 Verily, verily, I say unto you, He that entereth not by the door into the sheepfold, but climbeth up some other way, the same is a thief and a robber.
2 But he that entereth in by the door is the shepherd of the sheep.
3 To him the porter openeth; and the sheep hear his voice: and he calleth his own sheep by name, and leadeth them out.
4 And when he putteth forth his own sheep, he goeth before them, and the sheep follow him: for they know his voice.

---

* See Biblical Antiquities, Part II., ch. 3, sec. 3.

INSTRUCTIONS OF THE SAVIOUR.

5 And a stranger will they not follow, but will flee from him; for they know not the voice of strangers.
6 This parable spake Jesus unto them: but they understood not what things they were which he spake unto them.
7 Then said Jesus unto them again, Verily, verily, I say unto you, I am the door of the sheep.
8 All that ever came before me are thieves and robbers: but the sheep did not hear them.
9 I am the door: by me if any man enter in, he shall be saved, and shall go in and out, and find pasture.
10 The thief cometh not, but for to steal, and to kill, and to destroy: I am come that they might have life, and that they might have it more abundantly.
11 I am the good shepherd: the good shepherd giveth his life for the sheep.
12 But he that is a hireling, and not the shepherd, whose own the sheep are not, seeth the wolf coming, and leaveth the sheep, and fleeth; and the wolf catcheth them, and scattereth the sheep.
13 The hireling fleeth, because he is a hireling, and careth not for the sheep.
14 I am the good shepherd, and know my *sheep*, and am known of mine.
15 As the Father knoweth me, even so know I the Father: and I lay down my life for the sheep.
16 And other sheep I have, which are not of this fold: them also I must bring, and they shall hear my voice; and there shall be one fold, *and* one shepherd.
17 Therefore doth my Father love me, because I lay down my life, that I might take it again.
18 No man taketh it from me, but I lay it down of myself. I have power to lay it down, and I have power to take it again. This commandment have I received of my Father.

1. WHAT did Jesus say?
To whom does this seem to have been said?—John ix. 40.
What is a sheepfold? (A place where sheep are collected.)
What did Christ mean to speak of under that name? (His Church.)
Can you mention any texts in which God's people are compared to a flock, and the Lord to a shepherd?—Ps. lxxx. 1; Heb. xiii. 20; 1 Peter ii. 25.
What is meant by the door?—See ver. 7.
How may Christ be said to be the door of this sheepfold? (It is only entered through faith in him.)
What did Christ say of those who did not enter by the door?
How are such like robbers getting into a sheepfold? (They do not enter in the right way or for good purposes.)
Who are represented by this?—See ver. 8.
How did this apply to the Pharisees? (They claimed to be religious teachers, but they misled and oppressed the people to aggrandize themselves.)

2. Who is he that entereth in by the door?
Who is the shepherd?—See ver. 11.
How can Jesus be said to be both the door and the shepherd? (His atonement provides a way of salvation, and he is the guide and protector of his people.
What is it to enter by the door? (To trust in Jesus for our salvation.)

3. Who opens to the shepherd?
Who hears his voice?

What does he do for his sheep?
What is a *porter?* (A doorkeeper.)
What is meant by the sheep *hearing* his voice? (Obeying it.)

4. What is said of the shepherd when he putteth forth his sheep?
Why do the sheep follow him?
What is meant by *putting forth* his sheep? (Leading them.)
Did the shepherds in ancient times drive their sheep before them! (No; they went before, and the sheep followed them.)
How does Jesus lead his people? (By his example.)

5. Whom will the sheep not follow?
Who is meant by a *stranger?* (A false teacher.)
Why will they not follow him?—Prov. xix. 27.
What is the character of ministers who rightly watch and feed the sheep of Christ?—1 Peter v. 2-4.

6. What is said of the Jews, when Jesus spoke this parable to them?

7. How did Jesus explain the parable?
What did our Lord mean by calling himself the *door* of the sheep? (Through faith in him they enter into eternal life.)
What did he tell his disciples?—John xiv. 6.

8. What did he say about those who came before him?
Who are here meant? (The scribes and Pharisees.)
How did the sheep receive them?
Of what did the apostle Paul bid the Colossians beware?—Col. ii. 8.

9. What did Jesus again declare himself to be?
What does he promise to him who enters in by the door?
Into what does our Saviour here speak of entering? (His Church.)
From what shall he be saved? (From eternal death.)
What blessings are meant by *going in and out and finding pasture?* (Spiritual blessing.)
How did David speak of them?—Ps. xxiii.

10. For what purpose does the thief come?
Who is meant by *the thief?* (False teachers.)
How does a false teacher *steal, and kill, and destroy?*—Matt. xv. 14; 1 Tim. vi. 3-5.
For what purpose did Jesus come?
That *who* might have life? (Those who believe in Jesus.)
What sort of life will he give them?—John iii. 16, 17.

11. Who is the good Shepherd?

What does the good Shepherd do for the sheep?
How did Jesus do this? (By his death on the cross.)
Why was it necessary for Jesus to give his life for his sheep?
—Isa. liii. 6.

12. What does the hireling do when he seeth the wolf coming?
Who is meant by an hireling? (An unfaithful mercenary minister.)
Whom did our Saviour once compare to wolves?—Matt. vii. 15.

13. Why does the hireling flee?

14. What did Jesus say about himself and his sheep?

15. What did Jesus say of himself and the Father?
How did Christ show his love?
When was this done?—Matt. xxvii.

16. What did Jesus say about his other sheep?
Whom did he mean by *this fold?* (The Jews.)
Who were the *others?* (Gentiles.)
How did the apostle write to Gentile Christians?—Eph. ii. 11-14.
What is meant by the words *there shall be one fold and one shepherd?* (The people of God are those who believe in Christ, without distinction of Jew or Gentile.)
What did the apostle say to the Corinthians about this?—1 Cor. xii. 13.
How then should Christians live?—See Eph. iv. 1-6.

17. Why does the Father love the Son?
How did Jesus, when he had laid down his life, take it again?
—Matt. xxviii. 1-7.

18. Could any man take his life from him?
As men did crucify the Lord Jesus, what did he mean by this? (That he gave his life willingly, or men could not have taken it.)
What had he power to do?
Of whom had he received this commandment?
What is meant by *this commandment?* (This appointment.)

LESSON XXXII.

Parable of the Nobleman's Kingdom and the Pounds.

LUKE xix. 11-27.

11 And as they heard these things, he added and spake a parable, because he was nigh to Jerusalem, and because they thought that the kingdom of God should immediately appear.

12 He said therefore, A certain nobleman went into a far country to receive for himself a kingdom, and to return.

13 And he called his ten servants, and delivered them ten pounds, and said unto them, Occupy till I come.

14 But his citizens hated him, and sent a message after him, saying, We will not have this man to reign over us.

15 And it came to pass, that when he was returned, having received the kingdom, then he commanded these servants to be called unto him, to whom he had given the money, that he might know how much every man had gained by trading.

16 Then came the first, saying, Lord, thy pound hath gained ten pounds.

17 And he said unto him, Well, thou good servant: because thou hast been faithful in a very little, have thou authority over ten cities.

18 And the second came, saying, Lord, thy pound hath gained five pounds.

19 And he said likewise to him, Be thou also over five cities.

20 And another came, saying, Lord, behold, *here is* thy pound, which I have kept laid up in a napkin:

21 For I feared thee, because thou art an austere man: thou takest up that thou layedst not down, and reapest that thou didst not sow.

22 And he saith unto him, Out of thine own mouth will I judge thee, *thou* wicked servant. Thou knewest that I was an austere man, taking up that I laid not down, and reaping that I did not sow:

23 Wherefore then gavest not thou my money into the bank, that at my coming I might have required mine own with usury?

24 And he said unto them that stood by, Take from him the pound, and give *it* to him that hath ten pounds.

25 (And they said unto him, Lord, he hath ten pounds.)

26 For I say unto you, That unto every one which hath shall be given; and from him that hath not, even that he hath shall be taken away from him.

27 But those mine enemies, which would not that I should reign over them, bring hither, and slay *them* before me.

11. WHY did our Lord speak this parable?
Why did they expect that Christ would become a king at Jerusalem? (It was the capital of Judea.)
For what was he going to Jerusalem?—Matt. xx. 17-19.

12. How does the parable begin?
Who is represented by this nobleman? (Jesus Christ.)
What did the nobleman go away for?

13. What did he first do with his servants?
What did he say to them?
What is meant by *occupy till I come?* (Use what I have given you profitably.)
What is given to each one of us to improve?
How long will we have the opportunity of improving what God has given to us? (Till he comes to call us to die.)
Do we know when he will come?

INSTRUCTIONS OF THE SAVIOUR. 99

14. Who hated the nobleman?
Who are meant by his citizens? (His subjects.)
What message did they send after him?
How did the Jews feel towards Christ?—John viii. 40, 59.
Why did they hate him?—John vii. 7.
What do you learn concerning their treatment of him in John i. 11?
Do none but the Jews reject Christ, and desire that he should not reign over them? (All impenitent sinners do so.)
When you choose your own ways contrary to God's word, what do you, in effect, say?
Have sinners any excuse for rejecting Jesus? (No.—1 Tim. i. 15; Luke ii. 10, 11.

15. When the nobleman returned, what did he command respecting the servants?
Had he received the kingdom?
Will the opposition of sinners prevent Christ from reigning? (No.—1 Cor. xv. 25; Rev. xix. 16.)
Why did he command the servants to be called to him?
When will all men be brought to such an account? (At the judgment.)
Have we any assurance that *more* time will be given us to prepare?—James iv. 14.
Of what shall we all give an account at the day of judgment?—Eccles. xii. 14.

16. What did the first servant say?
Did he ascribe any glory to himself? (No.)
What will all Christ's faithful servants be ready to say?—Ps. cxv. 1.

17. What did the nobleman say to this servant?
Why did he call him a *good* servant? (He had been faithful to his duty.)
What kind of people will Jesus address at the last day, as having been good servants?—Rom. ii. 7.
What will he say to them?—Matt. xxv. 34.

18. What did the second servant say?

19. What did his Lord say to him?
Why did he not receive ten cities as well as the first? (The reward was according to each one's faithfulness.)
What is written in Rev. xxii. 12?
What is represented by one servant gaining more than another? (One was more devoted to his master's service than the other.)

20. What did another say?

21. Why had he not traded with it?

What is an *austere* man? (Severe, oppressive.)
Is the Lord an austere master? (No.—Matt. xi. 30; Ps. cxlv. 9.)
What is the meaning of the rest of his speech? (That his master was exacting and unjust.)
Who gives us every means of doing good and glorifying God?—Acts xvii. 24, 25.
Can we say then that the Lord expects to reap where he has not sown?—1 Chron. xxix. 11-14.
What sort of people are like this servant? (Impenitent sinners.)
Why do sinners think the Lord a hard master? (God requires what they are unwilling to do.)

22, 23. What did the nobleman say to this servant?
How did he judge him *out of his own mouth?* (By his own words.)
If he had really thought of his lord, as he said, what would he have done with his money?
What is meant by *giving his money into the bank?* (Placing it at interest.)
What is *usury?* (Interest.)
Will the excuses of those who make no use of the talents God gives them, be accepted?—Matt. xxv. 41-46.

24. What did the nobleman say to them that stood by?
Why was it given to *him?* (Because he had been faithful to his own charge.)

25. What did they that stood by say to him?

26. What did the nobleman say?
How may this be applied to the manner in which the Lord will treat men? (God will increase the means of usefulness to those who have a disposition to improve them.)

27. What command did the king give respecting his enemies?
Who were they?—Ver. 14.
Whom does our Lord Jesus Christ consider as his enemies?—Matt. xii. 30.
How do people show that they will not have Christ to reign over them? (By refusing or neglecting to obey him.)
Why are they unwilling that he should reign over them?—Rom. viii. 7.
How will they be punished at last?—2 Thess. i. 8, 9.
What parable is recorded by Matthew like this?—See Matt. xxv. 14-30.
What was the bad servant's punishment in that parable?—Matt. xxv. 30.
Who are the unprofitable servants of the Lord?—Luke xii. 47

INSTRUCTIONS OF THE SAVIOUR.

LESSON XXXIII.

Parables of the Two Sons and the Wicked Husbandmen.

MATT xxi. 28–46.

28 ¶ But what think ye? A *certain* man had two sons; and he came to the first, and said, Son, go work to-day in my vineyard.
29 He answered and said, I will not: but afterward he repented, and went.
30 And he came to the second, and said likewise. And he answered and said, I *go*, sir; and went not.
31 Whether of them twain did the will of *his* father? They say unto him, The first. Jesus saith unto them, Verily I say unto you, That the publicans and the harlots go into the kingdom of God before you.
32 For John came unto you in the way of righteousness, and ye believed him not: but the publicans and the harlots believed him: and ye, when ye had seen *it*, repented not afterward, that ye might believe him.
33 ¶ Hear another parable: There was a certain householder, which planted a vineyard, and hedged it round about, and digged a wine-press in it, and built a tower, and let it out to husbandmen, and went into a far country:
34 And when the time of the fruit drew near, he sent his servants to the husbandmen, that they might receive the fruits of it.
35 And the husbandmen took his servants, and beat one, and killed another, and stoned another.
36 Again, he sent other servants more than the first: and they did unto them likewise.
37 But last of all he sent unto them his son, saying, They will reverence my son.
38 But when the husbandmen saw the son, they said among themselves, This is the heir; come, let us kill him, and let us seize on his inheritance.
39 And they caught him, and cast *him* out of the vineyard, and slew *him*.
40 When the lord therefore of the vineyard cometh, what will he do unto those husbandmen?
41 They say unto him, He will miserably destroy those wicked men, and will let out *his* vineyard unto other husbandmen, which shall render him the fruits in their seasons.
42 Jesus saith unto them, Did ye never read in the Scriptures, The stone which the builders rejected, the same is become the head of the corner: this is the Lord's doing, and it is marvellous in our eyes?
43 Therefore say I unto you, The kingdom of God shall be taken from you, and given to a nation bringing forth the fruits thereof.
44 And whosoever shall fall on this stone shall be broken: but on whomsoever it shall fall, it will grind him to powder.
45 And when the chief priests and Pharisees had heard his parables, they perceived that he spake of them.
46 But when they sought to lay hands on him, they feared the multitude, because they took him for a prophet.

WHERE was Jesus when he spoke this parable?—See ver. 23.
To whom did he tell it?—See ver. 23.

28. How did he call their attention to what he was going to say?
Who are the persons of the parable?
What did he say to the first son?
What is a *vineyard?* (An inclosure for cultivating grapes.)

29. How did the son answer his father?
What did he afterwards do?

Whose conduct did our Lord mean to represent by this? (The publicans and openly wicked persons.)
What was wrong in this conduct? (Refusing at first.)
What was right in it? (Repenting and obeying.)
What sort of people are like this son? (Those who repent of their wickedness and forsake it.)

30. What did the man say to his second son?
What is meant by, *he said likewise?* (He said to him what he had said to the other.)
What did the second son say?
What is meant by, *I go, sir?* (I will do as you desire.)
Did he go?
Whom did the Lord mean by the second son? (The Pharisees.)
What is said of the scribes and Pharisees in Matt. xxiii. 3?
What was said of the Jews of old?—Ezek. xxxiii. 31.
What sort of people now are like them? (These who are only outwardly religious.)

31. What question did Jesus ask them?
What is the meaning of *twain?* (Two.)
What was the will of his Father?—Verse xxviii.
How did they answer Jesus?
What was the conduct of the first? (He repented and obeyed.)
Why was the first son better than the other? (He obeyed and the other did not.)
Which is better, to repent of sin and obey God, or to promise that we will obey him, and not do it.)
What did Jesus then say to the Jews?
What is meant by the publicans and harlots going into the kingdom of God before them? (They were more likely to become Christians.)

32. Why would this happen?
What John was meant? (John the Baptist.)
How was this like the conduct of the man's second son? (They professed to obey God, but refused to believe what John was sent to teach them.)
Did not the Jews profess to serve God more than any other people did? (Yes.—Rom. ii. 17-19.)
How then were they like the son who said "I go, sir," but went not? (Their profession was insincere.)
What especially did John say which they did not believe?—John i. 20, 30.
What conversation took place between our Lord and the Jews which led to the parable of the two sons?—Ver. 23-27.
Who believed John?
How were the publicans and harlots then like the first? (They repented and believed.)
Were the publicans Jews? (Yes.)

INSTRUCTIONS OF THE SAVIOUR. 103

Had they *professed* to obey God before? (No.)
How then were they like the son who said, "I will not," but afterwards repented and went? (By their wicked lives they had refused to obey God, but they repented and believed the Gospel.)
What did Jesus tell the chief priests and elders of their conduct?

33. What did Jesus then bid them hear?
What is the parable about?
What is meant by *hedging* a vineyard, digging a wine-press, &c.?*
To whom did he then let it, and where did he go?
What were the husbandmen to do? (To cultivate it.)
Who is meant by this householder? (God.)
What nation is represented by the vineyard?—Isa. v. 7.
What were the Lord's special acts of mercy to the Jews?—Rom. ix. 4, 5.
Who are meant by the husbandmen to whom the vineyard was let? (The Jews.)
Who, in these days, share all these privileges? (The Gentiles.)

34. When the time of the fruit drew near, what did the householder do?
What reason had he to expect fruit? (He had taken great care for its cultivation.)
Who are probably meant by the servants sent to the husbandmen?—Jer. xxv. 4.
What fruit did God expect from them?—Deut. xxvi. 27; Isa. xliii. 21.
What has he done for you?
What has he a right to expect from you?

35. How did the husbandmen treat the servants?
How were many of the prophets treated?—See Heb. xi. 37.

36. What did the householder again do?
How did they treat them?
How do ungodly men now sometimes show their hatred of the Lord's ministers and of their master?

37. Whom did the householder send last of all?
What did he say?
How is he spoken of in the account given by Mark?—Mark xii. 6.
Who is meant by his son? (Our Lord Jesus Christ.)
What is written in Heb. i. 1, 2?
What is the meaning of *reverence?* (To respect and honour.)

---

* See Biblical Antiquities, Part I., ch. 4, sec. 2.

38. When the husbandmen saw the son what did they say among themselves?
What is an *heir?* (One who inherits property.)
What is an *inheritance?* (Property to which an heir succeeds.)

39. What did the husbandmen do to the son of their lord?
What did the Jews do to Jesus?—Matt. xxvii.
What did Stephen say to the Jews?—Acts vii. 52.

40. What question did our Lord then ask?

41. How did the Jews answer Jesus?
Did they understand what Jesus meant? (Not yet.)
How does it apply to the coming of the Lord Jesus?—Jude 14, 15.

42. What did Jesus then ask them?
In what part of the Scriptures is this written?—Ps. cxviii. 22, 23.
Who is meant by this stone? (Jesus Christ.—Isa. xxviii. 16.)
Who are meant by the builders? (The Jews.)
Why is Christ called the corner-stone? (He is that sure foundation on which his church rests.)

43. What did Jesus farther say to them?
Whom did he show them here that he meant by the wicked husbandmen? (The Jewish nation.)
What nation did he mean to whom it should be given?—Acts xxviii. 28.
Have we any concern in this? (Yes: we are Gentiles.)
If we do not bring forth the right fruit, what is written concerning us in Rom. xi. 21, 22.

44. What did Jesus say of whomsoever should fall on that stone?
What is said in explanation of this, in 1 Pet. ii. 8?
What shall be the doom of him on whom it shall fall?
On whom shall it fall? (On those who reject Christ.)

45. When the chief priests and Pharisees had heard his parables, what did they perceive?
Why did they understand more fully now?—Ver. 43.

46. Why did they not lay hands on him?
For what did the multitude take Jesus?
What would they probably have done if the chief priests and Pharisees had taken him?—John xi. 53.
Whom did their seeking to kill him prove him to be?—Ver. 38.

LESSON XXXIV.

The Wedding Garment.

MATT. xxii. 1-14.

1 And Jesus answered and spake unto them again by parables, and said,
2 The kingdom of heaven is like unto a certain king, which made a marriage for his son,
3 And sent forth his servants to call them that were bidden to the wedding: and they would not come.
4 Again, he sent forth other servants, saying, Tell them which are bidden, Behold, I have prepared my dinner: my oxen and *my* fatlings *are* killed, and all things *are* ready: come unto the marriage.
5 But they made light of *it*, and went their ways, one to his farm, another to his merchandise:
6 And the remnant took his servants, and entreated *them* spitefully, and slew *them*.
7 But when the king heard *thereof*, he was wroth: and he sent forth his armies, and destroyed those murderers, and burned up their city.
8 Then saith he to his servants, The wedding is ready, but they which were bidden were not worthy.
9 Go ye therefore into the highways, and as many as ye shall find, bid to the marriage.
10 So those servants went out into the highways, and gathered together all as many as they found, both bad and good: and the wedding was furnished with guests.
11 ¶ And when the king came in to see the guests, he saw there a man which had not on a wedding garment:
12 And he saith unto him, Friend, how camest thou in hither not having a wedding garment? And he was speechless.
13 Then said the king to the servants, Bind him hand and foot, and take him away, and cast *him* into outer darkness; there shall be weeping and gnashing of teeth.
14 For many are called, but few *are* chosen.

1. How did Jesus again speak to the people?
What parables had he just spoken to them?
Why did our Lord give so many of his instructions by parables? (To impress more forcibly the truths he taught.)

2. What did he say of the kingdom of heaven?
What does this represent? (The giving of the Gospel.)

3. What did the king do?
Who are represented by the servants of the king? (Those who preach the Gospel.)
Who were first called by the Gospel?—Acts iii. 25, 26.
How did they treat the call?
Who treat the Gospel now as those persons did the invitation to the wedding? (Impenitent sinners.)
What did our Lord himself say to the Jews?—John v. 40.
Why will not men come to Christ?—Rom. viii. 7.

4. What did the king do then?
How is this like the Gospel? (Its offers are repeated to those who reject them.)
How often are sinners entreated to come to Christ? (Whenever, by any means, their attention is called to his salvation.)

How is every thing *prepared* for them? (Jesus has made a full atonement for all sin.)
What were they to tell those who had been bidden?
What moved God to prepare this provision for perishing sinners?—John iii. 16.

5. How did those who were bidden treat the second message?
What is meant by their making light of it? (Treating it as being unimportant.)
How do men now make light of the Gospel message? (By neglecting it.)
How did they show their neglect of it?
How are you cautioned against the love of worldly things in 1 John ii. 15?
What is written in Luke viii. 14?

6. How did some of them treat the king's servants?
Whose conduct does this represent? (Those who ill-treat God's messengers.)
Whom did the Jews treat spitefully and slay?—Acts vii. 52; 1 Thess. ii. 15.
How did the Jews treat Stephen when he was sent to preach to them?—Acts vii. 58.

7. When the king heard of it, how was he affected?
What is the meaning of *wroth?* (Very angry.)
What did he do?
How did this apply to what happened to Jerusalem? (They had murdered the prophets, and God destroyed their city.)
Repeat the words of the Lord Jesus concerning Jerusalem in Luke xix. 41-44.
What armies did God send against Jerusalem? (The Roman.)
Can you tell any thing about the destruction of that city, and the punishment of the Jews? (In A. D. 70, the city and temple were demolished, and the Jews have been dispersed among other nations.)
What may those expect who, in these days, make light of God's message, or persecute his servants?—Prov. xxix. 1.

8. What did the king then say to his servants?
Of what were they not worthy? (Of being the king's guests.)
Why were they not worthy? (They had rejected his invitation.)

9. What did the king therefore bid his servants do?
What are *highways?* (Public roads.)
What is meant by the king's sending his servants to those in highways? (The invitation was given to all, without distinction.)
What did Paul and Barnabas say to the Jews?—Acts xiii. 46.

INSTRUCTIONS OF THE SAVIOUR. 107

Who were now to be bidden?
How is the preaching of the Gospel like this?—Rev. xxii. 17.

10. Where did the servants go, and what did they do?
What are *guests?* (Persons entertained in the house of another.)
How did the Gentiles receive the Gospel?—Acts xxviii. 28.
What may be understood by the good and bad being gathered to the feast? (All kinds of people.)

11. Whom did the king see when he came in
What custom at weddings is alluded to here?*
Who may be said to come to the Gospel without a wedding garment? (Hypocritical professors.)
Is it enough to call ourselves Christians, if our hearts are not changed? (No.—John iii. 3.)
How alone can sinners be made fit for heaven?—Rev. iii. 18.

12. What did the king say to this man?
What may *we* learn from this? (That God sees us as we are.)
What is written concerning the New Jerusalem in Rev. xxi. 27?
What is said of the man when the king spoke thus to him?
Why probably was he speechless? (He knew he had no excuse.)
What excuse can *you* offer, if you ⸺ e found in the day of judgment not prepared to meet God?

13. What did the king say to his servants?
What is meant by *outer darkness?* (Complete darkness.)
What do you learn in Matt. xiii. 41, 42?
Why shall there be weeping and gnashing of teeth? (Because of the hopeless anguish, the despairing grief.)

14. What is added in this verse?
How was this with respect to the Jews?—See ver. 3.
How is it with respect to many others?—See ver. 11.
What is the call in Isa. xlv. 22?
What sort of people are chosen?—Ps. lv. 3.
Have you been called?
Have you obeyed the call of the Gospel?

---

*See Biblical Antiquities, Part I., chap. 6, sec. 1.

LESSON XXXV.

Parable of the Ten Virgins.

MATT. xxv. 1–13.

1 Then shall the kingdom of heaven be likened unto ten virgins, which took their lamps, and went forth to meet the bridegroom.
2 And five of them were wise, and five were foolish.
3 They that were foolish took their lamps, and took no oil with them:
4 But the wise took oil in their vessels with their lamps.
5 While the bridegroom tarried, they all slumbered and slept.
6 And at midnight there was a cry made, Behold the bridegroom cometh; go ye out to meet him.
7 Then all those virgins arose, and trimmed their lamps.
8 And the foolish said unto the wise, Give us of your oil; for our lamps are gone out.
9 But the wise answered, saying, Not so; lest there be not enough for us and you: but go ye rather to them that sell, and buy for yourselves.
10 And while they went to buy, the bridegroom came; and they that were ready went in with him to the marriage: and the door was shut.
11 Afterward came also the other virgins, saying, Lord, Lord, open to us.
12 But he answered and said, Verily I say unto you, I know you not.
13 Watch therefore; for ye know neither the day nor the hour wherein the Son of man cometh.

1. To what did our Lord say the kingdom of heaven should *then* be likened?
What had he been talking to them about, and what time did he mean by *then?* (His coming at the day of judgment.)
What is meant in *this* place by *the kingdom of heaven?* (Christ's second coming.)
What is a *bridegroom?* (A man newly married.)
To what customs among the Jews did Jesus allude? (To their wedding customs.)
Who is meant by the bridegroom? (Jesus Christ.)

2. What is said of these virgins?
Who are represented by the wise and foolish virgins? (Sincere and insincere professors of religion.)

3. What is said about the foolish virgins?
Why should they have taken oil with them? (Their lamps would not burn without it.)

4. What did the wise virgins do?
Who are meant by the wise virgins? (True Christians.)
What is signified by their having oil in their vessels with their lamps? (They were ready for the coming of the Lord.)
Why are those wise who prepare for the future?—1 Chron. xxix. 15.

5. What did they all do while the bridegroom tarried?
What is the meaning of *tarried?* (Delayed.)
What does the apostle Paul say to Christians in 1 Thess. v. 5–8?

6. What cry was made at midnight?

INSTRUCTIONS OF THE SAVIOUR. 109

What part of the wedding customs is here alluded to? (The sending a messenger to announce the coming of the bridegroom.)
How does this apply to the coming of the Lord Jesus? (It will be sudden,—to many, unexpected.)
Do any of us know when *we* shall hear that cry?
How shall you be *prepared* to meet the Lord?—Acts xvi. 31; Gal. vi. 7, 8.
When must you prepare?—2 Cor. vi. 2; Eccles. ix. 10.
Why is it necessary to be ready before you are called?
What is written in Luke xii. 40?

7. What did the virgins do when they heard the cry?
Why did they begin to trim their lamps? (To have them burn well.)

8. What did the foolish say to the wise?
What had happened to them?
Why did they want oil now? (They wanted their lamps to burn, because they were called to go.)
How is this like the condition of sinners who have not prepared to meet Christ?
Can the wise do them any good then? (They cannot give them the pardon of sin.)

9. How did the wise virgins answer them?
To whom must the Christian direct the dying sinner for pardon? (To our Saviour.)
What are the words of Jesus in Rev. iii. 18?

10. What took place while they went to buy?
Who went in with him?
What was done then?
Who were those that were ready? (The wise.)
Why was the door shut? (No more would be admitted to the feast.)
Against whom will the door of mercy be for ever shut? (Against those who die unprepared.)
What is written in Rev. iii. 7?
Are we sure of having any other season but the present to prepare to meet Christ?—Prov. xxvii. 1.

11. What did the foolish do afterwards?
How is the conduct of impenitent sinners often like this? (They ask for mercy without seeking it by faith in Christ.)

12. How were they answered?
What is written in Luke xiii. 24, 25?
When will it be too late for the wicked to obtain mercy? (After death.)
Repeat Isa. lv. 6, and Prov. i. 28-31?

How was Esau treated when it was too late for him to inherit the blessing?—Heb. xii. 17.

13. What did Jesus therefore tell them to do?
What is it to watch? (To be prepared.)
Why should they watch?
What is meant by the coming of the Son of man? (His coming to judge the world.)
Do you know when he will come to call you into eternity?
What must be your character to be ready to meet Christ?

LESSON XXXVI.

Parable of the Talents.

WHAT was the subject of the last lesson?
What was the advice of our Lord to his disciples?—Ver. 13.

MATT. xxv. 14–30.

14 ¶ For *the kingdom of heaven is* as a man travelling into a far country, *who* called his own servants, and delivered unto them his goods.
15 And unto one he gave five talents, to another two, and to another one; to every man according to his several ability; and straightway took his journey.
16 Then he that had received the five talents went and traded with the same, and made *them* other five talents.
17 And likewise he that *had received* two, he also gained other two.
18 But he that had received one went and digged in the earth, and hid his lord's money.
19 After a long time the lord of those servants cometh, and reckoneth with them.
20 And so he that had received five talents came and brought other five talents, saying, Lord, thou deliveredst unto me five talents: behold, I have gained beside them five talents more.
21 His lord said unto him, Well done, *thou* good and faithful servant: thou hast been faithful over a few things, I will make thee ruler over many things: enter thou into the joy of thy lord.
22 He also that had received two talents came and said, Lord, thou deliveredst unto me two talents: behold, I have gained two other talents besides them.
23 His lord said unto him, Well done, good and faithful servant: thou hast been faithful over a few things, I will make thee ruler over many things: enter thou into the joy of thy lord.
24 Then he which had received the one talent came and said, Lord, I knew thee that thou art a hard man, reaping where thou hast not sown, and gathering where thou hast not strawed:
25 And I was afraid, and went and hid thy talent in the earth: lo, *there* thou hast *that* is thine.
26 His lord answered and said unto him, *Thou* wicked and slothful servant, thou knewest that I reap where I sowed not, and gather where I have not strawed:
27 Thou oughtest therefore to have put my money to the exchangers, and *then* at my coming I should have received mine own with usury.
28 Take therefore the talent from him, and give *it* unto him which hath ten talents.
29 For unto every one that hath shall be given, and he shall have abundance: but from him that hath not shall be taken away even that which he hath.
30 And cast ye the unprofitable servant into outer darkness: there shall be weeping and gnashing of teeth.

INSTRUCTIONS OF THE SAVIOUR. 111

14. What did he then say?
Who is represented by this man? (Our Lord Jesus Christ.)
Who are his servants? (Those who profess to be Christians.)
What are signified by the goods which the Lord delivers to his servants? (Their capabilities and opportunities of doing good.)
What has Christ given *you* which you ought to improve?

15. How did the man distribute his goods?
Were there Greek and Jewish gold and silver talents? (Yes.)
Why did he give more money to one than to another?
What is meant by his *several ability?* (The ability of each one.)
What did he do then?
What is the meaning of *straightway?* (Immediately.)
What were the servants to do with the talents? (To employ them usefully.)
From whom do men receive all that they have?—James i. 17.
What has the Lord a right to expect from us all?—Deut. x. 12.

16. What is said of him that had received five talents?
Who are those who may be said to have five talents committed to them? (Those who have the greatest power of doing good.)
How are they to use them? (For the glory of God.)
Where shall we find sure directions how to use the means which God gives us?—Ps. cxix. 105.
If a man has *influence* with his fellow-men, for instance, how ought he to use it? (In leading them to love God.)
If he has property, how should he employ it? (In spreading the Gospel.)
If he has time, or any other means of serving God, how should he employ them?—1 Peter iv. 10, 11.
If he has the means of knowing the will of the Lord, and of becoming more holy, how is he bound to use them? (Diligently.—2 Peter i. 5-8.)

17. What had he gained who had received two talents?

18. What was the conduct of the servant who had received *one* talent?
What should he have done? (Used profitably what he had.)
What sort of people are like this man? (Those who neglect their opportunities to do good because they are not so great as those of others.)
Does the Lord expect nothing from those who have but one talent?—2 Cor. viii. 12.

19. After a long time, what happened?
What is meant by his *reckoning* with them? (Inquiring what they had done.)
What is represented by this? (The judgment.)

Repeat Rom. xiv. 12.
Before whose judgment-seat shall we all stand?—2 Cor. v. 10.
When shall the Lord come to reckon with us?—Matt. xxiv. 36.

20. What did he who had received five talents bring? What did he say?
How had he gained five talents more?—Verse 16.
Why had this servant no fear in meeting his lord? (He had been faithful to his trust.)

21. What did the master say to that servant?
What is it to be faithful? (To act with fidelity.)
What is meant by entering into the joy of his master? (Sharing in the entertainment and rejoicings at his return.)
What is the *joy of their Lord*, into which the faithful disciples of Christ shall enter? (Heaven.)
What encouragement do they find in Gal. vi. 9?
What will God render to those who have patiently continued in well doing?—Rom. ii. 7.

22. What did he say who had received two talents?

23. What did his master say to him?
Will the Lord reward men according to their faithfulness, whether they have little or much?—Rev. xx. 13.
How did Christ show this on one occasion?—See Mark xii. 41-44.
What did he say of the woman who could only show her love by anointing him?—Mark xiv. 8.

24. What did he who received one talent say he knew his Lord to be?
What did he mean by saying he reaped where he had not sown, and gathered where he had not strawed? (That he required more than he had a right to.)
What did the Jews of old say of God?—Ezek. xxxiii. 17.

25. What did this servant further say to his Lord?
Are not people who have but small means of serving God, apt to think that nothing is expected from them? (Yes.)
Are there any who have no means committed to them? (Not any.)
Upon whom did this servant lay the blame of his unfaithfulness? (Upon his master.)
Can any sinner say that God has given him nothing that he must give account for? (No; we have every one some talent committed to us, for which we must give account.)

26. What did the master call this servant?
What is the meaning of *slothful?* (Indolent.)
Why did he call him wicked and slothful? (He had thought his master's requirements hard, and would not comply with them.)

Had he done any grossly wicked act, or only *neglected his duty?* (Neglected his duty.)
What does that teach you?

27. What did his master say he ought to have done?
What are exchangers? (Money dealers.)
Why should he have put his master's money with *them?* (That he might have received interest.)
What does God expect from those who have small means and few opportunities?—Acts xi. 29; 2 Cor. ix. 6, 7.

28. What did the master command to be done with the money of the slothful servant?
Why was it taken from him? (He had not improved it.)
Why was it given to him who had ten talents? (To reward his faithfulness.)

29. What did our Lord say of every one that hath?
Every one that hath *what?* (A disposition to be faithful to his duties.)
What shall be taken from him that hath not? (That which he misimproved.)
Him that hath not *what?* (The disposition to fulfill his duties.)
What may you expect, then, if you neglect the time and opportunities God is now giving you.)

30. Where was the unprofitable servant to be cast?
What will be the punishment of the unprofitable servants of the Lord Jesus?—Matt. xxv. 30.

LESSON XXXVII.

The Last Judgment.

MATT. xxv. 31-46.

31 ¶ When the Son of man shall come in his glory, and all the holy angels with him, then shall he sit upon the throne of glory:
32 And before him shall be gathered all nations: and he shall separate them one from another, as a shepherd divideth *his* sheep from the goats:
33 And he shall set the sheep on his right hand, but the goats on the left.
34 Then shall the King say unto them on his right hand, Come, ye blessed of my Father, inherit the kingdom prepared for you from the foundation of the world:
35 For I was an hungred, and ye gave me meat: I was thirsty, and ye gave me drink: I was a stranger, and ye took me in:
36 Naked, and ye clothed me: I was sick, and ye visited me: I was in prison, and ye came unto me.
37 Then shall the righteous answer him, saying, Lord, when saw we thee an hungred, and fed *thee?* or thirsty, and gave *thee* drink?
38 When saw we thee a stranger, and took *thee* in? or naked, and clothed *thee?*
39 Or when saw we thee sick, or in prison, and came unto thee?
40 And the King shall answer and

say unto them, Verily I say unto you, Inasmuch as ye have done it unto one of the least of these my brethren, ye have done it unto me.

41 Then shall he say also unto them on the left hand, Depart from me, ye cursed, into everlasting fire, prepared for the devil and his angels:

42 For I was an hungred, and ye gave me no meat: I was thirsty, and ye gave me no drink:

43 I was a stranger, and ye took me not in: naked, and ye clothed me not:

sick, and in prison, and ye visited not.

44 Then shall they also answer him, saying, Lord, when saw we thee an hungred, or athirst, or a stranger, or naked, or sick, or in prison, and did not minister unto thee?

45 Then shall he answer them, saying, Verily I say unto you, Inasmuch as ye did it not to one of the least of these, ye did it not to me.

26 And these shall go away into everlasting punishment: but the righteous into life eternal.

31. WHAT great day is here spoken of?
How will the Son of man come?
Who is the Son of man? (Jesus Christ.)
What is the glory of Christ?—See John xvii. 5.
Who will be with him?
Where shall he sit?

32. Who shall be gathered before him?
Who are meant by *all nations?* (All mankind.)
Why shall all nations be gathered before him? (For judgment.)
Shall you be there at that day?
How shall the living and the dead be brought in that day to stand before the Son of man?—1 Cor. xv. 51, 52.
What do you read of those who have been drowned in the sea? —Rev. xx. 13.
What of those who have slept in the dust of the earth?—Dan. xii. 2.
What shall become of the earth?—2 Pet. iii. 10.
What shall the Son of man then do?
Who are meant by the *sheep?* (Christians.)
Who are meant by the *goats?* (The wicked.)
Why will he separate them? (Because their characters are different.)
How will he know the characters of each?—John ii. 24, 25.
What does Jesus, the Son of man, say of himself in Rev. ii. 23?
Shall wicked children and pious parents remain together on that day? (No.)
How long shall they be separated? (For ever.)

33. Where shall he place the sheep?
What is denoted by the *right hand?* (Favour.)
Have you reason to believe that *you* shall be among the righteous at the day of judgment?
Where shall he place the goats?
Why shall they be placed on the left hand? (Because they are rejected.)

34. What shall the King say to them on his right hand?

INSTRUCTIONS OF THE SAVIOUR. 115

Who is here called the King? (Our Lord Jesus Christ.)
What is written concerning Jesus in Rev. xix. 16?
Whom do you then suppose Jesus to be?—Isa. ix. 6.
Why are those on the right hand called the blessed of the Father?—1 Cor. ii. 9.
What is it to inherit? (To receive as a possession.)
Why is heaven called the *inheritance* of the righteous?—See Rom. viii. 16, 17.
What does the apostle Peter say of this inheritance?—1 Pet. i. 4, 5.
Has this kingdom been promised to the people of God?—Luke xii. 32.
What is meant by the *foundation* of the world?—Gen. i. 1.

35, 36. What reason is given for this?

37, 38, 39. How shall the righteous answer the King?

40. What shall the King answer and say to them?
Who are meant by the least of these his brethren? (The most lowly Christian.)
How is it doing a kindness to Christ if we do it to any of his disciples? (He will regard it so, if we do it for his sake.)
What is written in Heb. ii. 11, and Matt. xii. 50?
What is then your duty to the hungry, thirsty, and to the stranger?
What should you do for the naked, the sick, and those in prison?
Why should you in this manner help these people?—Acts. xx. 35.
What people especially should you be careful to relieve when in distress?—Gal. vi. 10.
How can these things be done *for Christ's sake?* (When they are done because we love him, and desire to please him.)
What are the words of Jesus to his people in Mark ix. 41.
Will the righteous then be taken to heaven for their good works?—Luke xvii. 10.
Why then will the good words of God's people be mentioned at the day of judgment?—1 John iii. 14, 17.
Is kindness to the poor always a sign of the grace of God in the heart? (No.)
What must be the motives for such kindness to make it such as the Lord will bless? (Love and obedience to Christ.)

41. What shall the Judge then say to them on the left hand?
Why must they depart?—Rev. xxi. 27; Ps. v. 4, 5.
From whom must they depart? (From Christ.)
With whom must they for ever after dwell?
How long will they dwell with them? (For ever.)

42, 43. How had they acted?

116 PARABLES AND OTHER

44. How will the wicked answer him?
45. How shall he answer them?
Whom does he mean by those on his right hand?
Why shall the actions of the wicked be brought forward in the day of judgment?—Rev. xx. 12.
How does their neglect of duties show that men are not fit for heaven?—1 John iv. 8.
46. Into what shall the wicked go away?
Who will be their companions there?—Rev. xxi. 8; 2 Pet. ii. 4.
What is meant by *everlasting* punishment? (Never-ending punishment.)
Shall the wicked ever be taken to heaven?—Luke xvi. 26.
Into what shall the righteous enter?
What is meant by life eternal? (Perfect happiness forever.)
Who has purchased this blessing?—Rom. v. 8, 21.
For whom has it been purchased?—John iii. 16.

LESSON XXXVIII.

The Vine and the Branches.

JOHN xv. 1-8.

1 I am the true vine, and my Father is the husbandman.
2 Every branch in me that beareth not fruit he taketh away: and every *branch* that beareth fruit, he purgeth it, that it may bring forth more fruit.
3 Now ye are clean through the word which I have spoken unto you.
4 Abide in me, and I in you. As the branch cannot bear fruit of itself, except it abide in the vine; no more can ye, except ye abide in me.
5 I am the vine, ye *are* the branches.
He that abideth in me, and I in him, the same bringeth forth much fruit; for without me ye can do nothing.
6 If a man abide not in me, he is cast forth as a branch, and is withered; and men gather them, and cast *them* into the fire, and they are burned.
7 If ye abide in me, and my words abide in you, ye shall ask what ye will, and it shall be done unto you.
8 Herein is my Father glorified, that ye bear much fruit; so ye shall be my disciples.

1. To what did Jesus liken himself?
What is a *vine?* (This means a grape vine.)
To what did he liken his Father?
What is a *husbandman?* (Here it is the man who took care of the vine.)
2. What did he say of the branches of the vine?
Who are meant by the branches?—See ver. 5.
What is meant by the disciples of Christ *bearing fruit?* (Leading holy lives.)

INSTRUCTIONS OF THE SAVIOUR. 117

What is the fruit that they bear?—Phil. i. 11.
What does the Father do with the branches that do not bear fruit?
Who are meant by these branches? (Those whose lives show that they are not united to Christ.)
Why does a vine-dresser cut off such branches? (They are useless.)
Why does God cut off such people? (They are injurious to others.)
What does God do with the branches that bear fruit?
Who are represented by these branches? (True Christians.)
What is meant by *purging* or purifying a branch? (Pruning it.)
How does the Lord purify Christians? (By taking away what hinders their growth in grace.)
How then may we know whether we are true Christians?—See 2 Pet. i. 5-8.

3. By what are the disciples of Christ purified?
What *word* is that? (The things he had taught them.)
How can the words of Christ be said to purify those who obey them?—Psalm xix. 7, 9.

4. What must those do who wish to serve God?
What is it to abide in Christ? (To have faith in him.)
What is it for Christ to abide in us? (To give us grace and strength.)
What did the apostle desire for the Ephesian Christians?—Eph. iii. 17-19.
Why must this be done?
Why must sinners depend on Christ for every thing?—Rom. vii. 8.
Why must they continue to do this as long as they live? (If they do not, they will be like branches severed from the vine.)
How is this to be done?—Heb. xii. 1, 2; 2 Pet. iii. 18.

5. What did Christ then say?
What is the proof that a person is a true believer in Christ?
Why is it necessary to depend on Christ?
How does this show that all persons must go to Christ if they desire to be saved?
How does it show that all Christians must depend on Christ for help and strength?
How does Christ do this for those who come to him?—See John xvi. 7. 13.

6. What will become of those who do not abide in Christ?
What is done with the unfruitful branches that are cut off from the vine?

What will be done with those who reject or forsake Christ?—John viii. 24.
How did Christ once speak of this?—Matt. xiii. 40-42.

7. What is promised to those who abide in Christ and obey his word?

What kind of *asking* is meant? (The prayers of his believing, obedient followers.)
What did Jesus afterwards tell his disciples?—John xvi. 24.
Is this promise given to all the true disciples of Christ? (Yes.—Psalm cxlv. 18.)

8. How is the Father glorified?

What is the meaning of *glorified?* (Honoured.)
How does the fruitfulness of Christians glorify God?—Phil. ii. 13.
What is one of the ways in which this is done?—Matt. v. 16.
How does such conduct show that men are Christ's *disciples?* (It shows they have learned of him, and follow his example.)
If then a person does not glorify God by his piety and his good works, can he be a disciple of Christ?—Rom. viii. 9.
What did the Lord himself say to such?—Matt. xxv. 30.
In what ways may the young produce fruit to the glory of God?
What must they and all others remember in their attempts to be useful, and to increase in piety?—See ver. 4.

CONTENTS.

Lesson.		Page.
1.	Christ's conversation with Nicodemus.—John iii. 1-12.	7
2.	Christ's conversation with Nicodemus, continued.—John iii. 13-21.	9
3.	Jesus teaches the Nazarenes, and is rejected by them.—Luke iv. 16-30.	11
4.	The beginning of Christ's Sermon on the Mount.—Matt. v. 1-16.	14
5.	Christ came not to destroy the law—He teaches that it extends to the thoughts.—Matt. v. 17-30.	19
6.	Our Lord forbids swearing; teaches his people patiently to endure injuries, to love their enemies, and do good to all.—Matt. v. 33-48.	22
7.	Our Lord teaches how we should perform almsgiving, prayer, and fasting.—Matt. vi. 1-10.	26
8.	The Lord's Prayer, continued.—Matt. vi. 11-18.	29
9.	The Sermon on the Mount, continued.—Matt. vi. 19-34.	31
10.	The Sermon on the Mount, continued.—Matt. vii. 1-14.	35
11.	Conclusion of the Sermon on the Mount.—Matt. vii. 15-29.	38
12.	The Parable of the Sower.—Matt. xiii. 1-9, 18.	41
13.	Parables of the hidden treasure; the pearl of great price; and the net.—Matt. xiii. 44-58.	43
14.	Jesus teaches humility, and shows his care for his people by the parable of the lost sheep.—Matt. xviii. 1-14.	46
15.	Peter's question, How often he should forgive his brother—Christ's instruction about brotherly love.—Matt. xviii. 21-35.	50
16.	Jesus shows a certain lawyer, by the story of the good Samaritan, who is his neighbour.—Luke x. 25-37.	52
17.	Our Lord rebukes the wickedness of the Scribes and Pharisees.—Luke xi. 37-44.	55
18.	Subject continued.—Luke xi. 45-54.	57
19.	The Parable of the Tares.—Matt. xiii. 24-30. (36-43.)	59

CONTENTS.

LESSON.	PAGE.
20.—Jesus warns his disciples against hypocrisy and the fear of man.—The Parable of the covetous rich man.—Luke xii. 1-10. 15-21	61
21.—The duty of being ready for the coming of the Lord.—Luke xii. 35-48	65
22.—Christ warns the people to enter in at the strait gate, and laments over Jerusalem.—Luke xiii. 23-35	68
23.—The Parable of the Great Supper.—Luke xiv. 16-35	71
24.—Parable of the Prodigal Son.—Luke xv. 11-32	74
25.—Parable of the Unjust Steward.—Luke xvi. 1-17	77
26.—Parable of the Rich Man and Lazarus.—Luke xvi. 19-31.	81
27.—Jesus teaches his people to forgive one another, and shows the power of faith.—Luke xvii. 1-10	84
28.—The Parables of the Unjust Judge, and of the Pharisee and Publican.—Luke xviii. 1-14	86
29.—Jesus blesses little children, and discourses with a rich man on eternal life.—Matt. xix. 13-24	89
30.—Jesus teaches the Jews concerning himself.—John viii. 12-24	92
31.—Christ, the Good Shepherd.—John x. 1-18	94
32.—Parable of the Nobleman's Kingdom and the Pounds.—Luke xix. 11-27	98
33.—Parable of the Two Sons, and the Wicked Husbandmen.—Matt. xxi. 28-46	101
34.—The Wedding Garment.—Matt. xxi. 1-14	105
35.—Parable of the Ten Virgins.—Matt. xxv. 1-13	108
36.—Parable of the Talents.—Matt. xxv. 14-30	110
37.—The Last Judgment.—Matt. xxv. 31-46	113
38.—The Vine and the Branches.—John xv. 1-8	116

www.ingramcontent.com/pod-product-compliance
Lightning Source LLC
Chambersburg PA
CBHW020127170426
43199CB00009B/679